The Work of Christ

by

P.T. Forsyth

Copyright © 2017 Beloved Publishing
All rights reserved. No part of this book may be reproduced, scanned, or distributed in any printed or electronic form without permission.
Printed in the United States of America
ISBN: 978-1-63174-164-7

Preface

These chapters need to have it said that they were given as extempore lectures from rough notes to a gathering, largely of young ministers, in connection with Rev. Dr. Campbell Morgan's annual conference at Mundesley, Norfolk. They were taken down in shorthand and then carefully revised. They took place in July, 1909, immediately after the delivery of my Congregational Lecture on the *Person and Place of Christ*, which they supplement - especially when taken with my *Cruciality of the Cross* a few months before. It will be seen from the conditions that the book cannot pretend to be more than a higher kind of popularisation, though this is less true of the two last chapters, which have been more worked over. The style approaches in parts a conversational familiarity which would have been out of place in addressing theological experts. And as some of the ideas are unfamiliar I have not been too careful to avoid repetition. My hope is to be of some use to those ministers who are still at a stage when they are seeking more footing on such matters than they have been provided with in mere Biblical or Historical Theology. There is no region where religion becomes so quickly theology as in dealing with the work of Christ. No doctrine takes us so straight to the heart of things, or so forces on us a discussion of the merits of the case, the dogmatic of it, as distinct from its scriptural or its ecclesiastical career. No doctrine draws so directly on the personal religion of sinful men, and none, therefore, is open to so much change in the course of the Church's thought upon its growing faith and life. Thus when we consider that here we are at once where the form may change most in time and yet the feet be most firmly set for eternity, we realize how difficult and delicate our task must be. And we are made to feel as if the due book on such a theme could only be written from behind the veil with the most precious blood that ever flowed in human veins.

We are in a time when a spirituality without positive content seems attractive to many minds. And the numbers may grow of those favouring an undogmatic Christianity which is without apostolic or evangelical substance, but cultivates a certain emulsion of sympathetic mysticism, intuitional belief, and benevolent action. Among lay minds of a devout and social but impatiently practical habit, this is not unlikely to spread; and particularly among those whose public interests get the upper hand of ethical and historical insight and denude their religion of most of the reflection it demands.

Upon undogmatic, undenominational religion no Church can live. With mere spirituality the Church has not much directly to do; it is but a subjective thing; and its favour with many may be but another phase of the uncomprehending popular reverence (not to say superstition) for the recluse religionist, the mysterious ecstatic, and the ascetic pietist. What Christian faith and the Christian Church have to do with is *holy* spirituality - the spirituality of the Holy Spirit of our Redemption. The Christian revelation is not "God is a spirit," nor is it "God is love." Each of these great words is now much used to discredit the more positive faith from whose midst

John wrote them down. Herein is love, not in affection but in propitiation (1 John 4:10). Would Paul ever have written 1 Cor. 13 if it had been revealed to him that it was going to be turned against Rom 3:25? And what would his language have been to those who abused that chapter so? Christian faith is neither spirituality nor charity. Its revelation is the holiness in judgment of the spiritual and loving God. Love if only divine as it is holy; and spirituality is Christian only as it meets the conditions of Holy Love in the way the Cross did, as the crisis of holy judgment and holy grace. If the Cross is not simply a manner of religion but the object of our religion and the site of revelation, then it stands there above all to effect God's holiness, and not to concentrate man's self-sacrifice. And except in the Cross we have no guarantee for the supreme thing, the divine thing, in God, which is the changeless reality and irresistible sovereignty of His Holy Love.

It is upon such faith alone, given by the Cross alone, that a Church can live - upon the faith that founded it - upon a positive New Testament Gospel. Of that Gospel the Church is the trustee. And the Church betrays its trust and throws its life and its Lord away when it says, "Be beautifully spiritual and believe as you like," or "Do blessed good and think as you please."

There is timely saying of that searching Christian genius Kierkegaard - the great and melancholy Dane in whom Hamlet was mastered by Christ:

"For long the tactics have been: use every means to move as many as you can - to move everybody if possible - to enter Christianity. Do not be too curious whether what they enter *is* Christianity. My tactics have been, with God's help, to use every means to make it clear what the demand of Christianity really is - if not one entered it."

The statement is extreme; but that way lies the Church's salvation - in its anti-Nicene relation to the world, its pre-Constantinian, non-established, relation to the world, and devotion to the Word. Society is hopeless except for the Church. And the Church has nothing to live on but the Cross that faces and overcomes the world. It cannot live on a cross which is on easy terms with the world as the apotheosis of all its aesthetic religion, or the classic of all its ethical intuition. The work of Christ, rightly understood, is the final spiritual condition of all the work we may aspire to do in converting society to the kingdom of God.

I. The Difference Between God's Sacrifice and Man's

What I am going to say is not directly unto edification, but indirectly it is so must certainly. Directly it is rather for that instruction which is a need in our Christian life as essential as edification. We cannot do without either. On the one hand instruction with no idea of edification at all becomes mere academical discourse. It may begin anywhere and it may end anywhere. On the other hand, edification without instruction very soon becomes a feeble and ineffective thing. I think a great many of us would be agreed that part of the poverty and weakness of the Church at the present moment is due to the fact that edification has been pursued to the neglect of instruction. We have been a little too prone to dwell upon the simple side of the gospel. All our capital is in small circulation. We have not put by a reserve, as it were. And therefore the simplicity itself has become unsettled and ineffectual, confused and confusing.

I ask your attention to certain aspects of our Christian faith which perhaps do not lie immediately upon the surface, but which are yet the condition of the Church's continued energy and success in the world. I suppose there is nobody here who does not believe in the Church. At any rate, what I propose to say will be said entirely from that standpoint. We believe in the Holy Catholic Church. My contention would be that, apart from such a position as I desire to bring to your notice - some real apostolic belief in the real work of Jesus Christ - apart from that no Church can continue to exist. That is the point of view which I take at the outset. The Church is precious, not in itself, but because of God's purpose with it. It is there because of what God has done for it. It is there, more particularly, because of what Christ has done, and done in history. It is there solely to serve the Gospel.

It is impossible not to observe at the present day that the Church is under a cloud. You cannot take any division of it, in any country of the world, without feeling that that is so. Therefore I will begin by making quite a bold statement; and I should be quite prepared, given time and opportunity, to devote a whole week to making it good. The statement is that the Church of Christ is the greatest and finest product of human history. It is the greatest thing in the universe. That is in complete defiance of the general view and tendency of society at the present moment. I say the Church is the greatest and finest product of human history; because it is not really a product of human history, but the product of the Holy Spirit within history. It stands for the new creation, the New Humanity, and it has that in trust. The man who has a slight acquaintance with history is ready to bridle at a statement like that. He says: "Consider what the Roman Church has done; consider how obscurantist many sections of the Protestant Church are; consider the ineffectual position of the Church in modern civilization - and what nonsense to talk about the Church as the greatest and finest product of human history!" True enough, the authority of the Church is failing in many quarters. And that does not mean only the external authority of what you might call a statutory Church, a great institutional Church, a great organized Church like Rome, for example. It means much more than that. It means that the authority of the whole Church is weakened in respect of the inward and spiritual matter which it contains and preaches, and which makes it what it is. The Church is there as the vehicle of the power of the Holy Ghost and of the authority of the saving God - a God, that is, who is saving not groups here and there, but the whole of human society. But a spiritual authority for man altogether is at a discount. Perhaps we have brought that in some measure upon ourselves. Perhaps, too, it was historically necessary. But, necessary or not, it is a matter of fact that our Protestantism has developed often into a masterless individualism which is as deadly to Christian life as an over-organized institution like Rome. Many spiritual people today find it difficult to make their choice between the two extremes. Without going into the historic causes of the situation, let us recognize the situation. Spiritual authority, especially that of the Church, is for the time being at a great discount.

The Church is valuable as the organ of Christian grace, and truth, and power. But what do we find offered us in place of the Church? Those who attack the Church most seriously, and disbelieve in it most thoroughly, are not proposing simply to level the Church to the ground in the sense of destroying any religious society. What they want to do is to put some other kind of society in the place of the Church. For they say, as we all say, that it is impossible for religion, certainly impossible for Christianity, to exist without a social body in which it is cultivated and has its effect. Therefore, those who are opposed to the Church most bitterly are yet not prepared to make a total desert. But they put all kinds of organizations, fancy organizations and fancy religions, in its place. Take the great movement in the direction of Socialism. Take the Socialist programs that you find so plentifully everywhere. What do these various organizations mean? What do all these organizations mean which profess to embody human brotherhood, and are represented by Trades Unions, Co-operation, Fraternities, Guilds, Socialism? What is it they all confess? That some social vehicle there must be. You cannot promote Anarchy itself without associations for the purpose. So that the very existence of these rival organizations is a confession of the one fundamental principle of the Church, namely, that the human ideal, that religion in the true sense of the word, cannot do without a social habitation. They put in their own way what we put in our way (and we think a better way), that there must be a Church builded together for a habitation of God in the Spirit. Our individualisms have been troubling and weakening us so much that everybody is looking away to some form of human life which shall have the advantages of individualism without its perils. The pietistic form of individualism did in its day great service. But it is out of date. Rationalistic individualism, again, taking shape in political radicalism, has done good work in its day. That also seems going out of date. The value of the new movement is its - shall I say - solidarity; which is a confession of that social, fraternal principle which finds its consummation really, and its power only, in the Church of Christ.

When we look at these rival organizations (and they are many, and some will occur to you which I have not named), we can, I think, gather most of them under one head. In contrast with the Church the various social forms that are offered to us today would build society upon a natural basis, the basis of natural brotherhood, natural humanity, natural goodness - on human nature. And the issue between the Church and the chief rivals of the Church is an issue between society upon this natural basis, and society upon a supernatural basis. Our Christian belief is based upon the work of Christ; and we hold that human society can only continue to exist in final unity upon that same supernatural basis. It is an issue, therefore, between human nature deified and human nature saved; between mere sympathy and faith - faith taken in a quite positive and definite sense. We think that a brotherhood of mere sympathy, however warm it can be at a particular moment, has no stay in it, no eternal promise. The eternal promise is with supernatural faith. Do you ever believe otherwise? I hope you have been so tempted; because having got over it you will be very much better for having gone through it. I wish much more of our belief had gone through troubled scenes and come to its rest; we should make far greater impression upon men if we gave them to feel we had fought our way to the peace and power we have. Well, were you ever tempted to believe that Christianity is just human nature at its best? That is the most powerful and dangerous plea that is put forward just now in challenge of our Christian position and Church. Is the Kingdom of God just our natural spirituality and altruism developed? Is it just the spirit of religion or self-sacrifice, which you often find in human nature, developed to its highest? Is that the Kingdom of God? I trust you believe not - that human nature is not capable, by all the finest sacrifices it might develop, of saving, or ensuring itself, and setting up the Kingdom of God. Take the best side of human nature, that side which moves men to unselfishness and sacrifice, the side that comes out in many a heroic battle, in the silent battles of our civilization, where the victims get no applause and no reputation for their heroism whatever. Take the best side of human nature, illustrated in every coalpit accident and every such thing, in countless quiet homes of poverty, where lives are being worked down to the bone and ground to death toiling and slaving for others. Take the vast mass of fatherhood and motherhood living for the children only. Take that best side of human nature, make the most of it, and then put this question: "How does man's noblest work differ from Christ's great work?" That is the question to which I desire to attract your attention today. How does man's best work differ from Christ's great work?

Let me begin with a story which was reported in the Belgian papers some years ago. Two passenger trains were coming in opposite directions at full speed. As they approached the station, it was found the levers would not work, owing to the frost, and the points could not be set to clear the trains of each other. A catastrophe seemed to be inevitable; when a signalman threw himself flat between the rails, and with his hands held the tie-rod in such a way that the points were properly set and kept; and he remained thus while the train thundered over him, in great danger of having his head carried away by the low-hung gear of the Westinghouse brake. When the train had passed, he quietly rose and returned to his work.

I offer you some reflections on this incident. It is the kind of incident that may be multiplied indefinitely. I offer you certain reflections, first, on some of its analogies with Christ's work, and secondly, on some of its differences.

1. This man, in a very true sense, died and rose again. His soul went through what he would have gone through if he had never risen from the track. He gave himself; and that is all a man can give at last. His deed had the moral value which it would have had if he had lost his life. He laid it down, but it did not please God to take it. Like Abraham's sacrifice of Isaac, it was complete and acceptable, even though not accepted. The man's rising from the ground - was it not really a resurrection from the dead? It was not simply a return to his post. He went back another man. He went back a heavenlier man. He had died and risen, just as if he had been called, and had gone, to God's presence - could he but remain there. This is a death and rising again possible to us all. If the death and resurrection of Jesus Christ do not end in producing that kind of thing amongst us, then it is not the power of God unto salvation. These moral deaths and resurrections are what make men of us. "In deaths oft." That is the first point.

2. The second point is this. Not one of the passengers in either of those trains knew until they read it what had been done for them, nor to whom they owed their lives. It is so with the whole world. Today it owes its existence, in a way it but poorly understands, to the death and resurrection of Jesus Christ. That is the permanent element in Christianity -the Cross and resurrection of Jesus Christ. And yet it is nothing to all them that pass by. Under the feet of those travelers in Belgium there had taken place one of those deeds that are the very soul and glory of life, and they had no idea of it. Perhaps some of them were at the very moment grumbling at the staff of the railway for some small grievance or other. It is useful to remember, when we are inclined to grumble thus, what an amount of devotion to duty goes to make it possible for us to travel as safely as we do - far more than can be acknowledged by the payment of a wage. These people were ploughing along in safety over one of the railway staff lying in a living grave. I say it is so with the whole civilized world. Its progress is like that of the train; it seldom stops to think that its safety is owing to a divine death and resurrection, much more than heroic. The safety of that train was not due to the mechanism. The mechanism had gone wrong. It was not due to organization, or to work done from fear of punishment. Heroic duty raised to martyrdom saved the whole train. And the world's progress is saved today because of a death and resurrection of which it knows little and mostly cares to know less. *"Propter Jesum non quoerimus Jesum."* The success of Christ hides Him. It is the death of Christ that is the chief condition of modern progress. It is not civilization that keeps civilization safe and progressive. It is that power which was in Jesus Christ and culminated in His death and resurrection. When people read the Bible, and get behind the Bible, and that principle comes home to them, it

may sometimes be like the shock that those travelers would receive when they read in the newspaper of their risk and deliverance.

3. Another point. And I am now coming on to the difference. This man died for people who would thrill with the sense of what they owed him as soon as they read about it. His act appeals to the instinct which is ready to spring to life in almost every breast. You felt the response at once when I told you the story. Some of you may have even felt it keenly. Do you ever feel as keenly about the devoted death of Christ? Perhaps you never have. You have believed it, of course, but it never came home to you and gripped you as the stories of the kind I instance do You see the difference between Christ's death and every case of human heroism. I am moving to answer that question I put a moment ago as to whether the development of the best in human nature would ever give us the work of Christ and the Kingdom of God. I have been illustrating one of the finest things in human nature, and I am asking whether, if that were multiplied indefinitely, we should yet have the effect which is produced by the death of Christ, or which is still to be produced by it in God's purpose. No, there is a difference between Christ's death and every case of heroism. Christ's was a death on behalf of people within whom the power of responding had to be created. Everybody thrills to that story I told you, and to every similar story. The power of response is lying there in the human heart ready - it only needs to be touched. There is in human nature a battery charged with admiration for such things; you have only to put your knuckle to it and out comes the spark. But when we are dealing with the death of Christ we are in another position. Christ's was a death on behalf of people in whom the power of responding had to be created. We are all afraid of death, and rise to the man who delivers us from it. But we are not afraid of that worse thing than death from which Christ came to deliver us. Christ's death was not a case of heroism simply, it was a case of redemption. It acted upon dull and dead hearts. It was a death which had to evoke a feeling not only latent but paralyzed, not only asleep but dead. What does Paul say? "While we were yet without strength, Christ died for us" - without power, without feeling, as the full meaning is.

Let me illustrate. Take a poet like Wordsworth. When he began to publish his poetry he was received, just as Browning was received later, with ridicule and contempt. The greatest critic of the time began an article in the leading critical organ of the day by saying, "This will never do." But it has done; and it has done for Jeffrey's critical reputation. Lord Jeffrey wrote himself down as one who was incapable of gauging the future, however much he might be capable of understanding the literature of the past. Some of you may remember - I remember perfectly well - the same kind of thing in the penny papers about Browning when he was fighting for recognition. I remember, when I was a student, reading articles in luminaries like *The Standard* which sneered and jeered at Browning, just as smaller men today would sneer at men of like originality. But Wordsworth and Browning have conquered. I take another case. Turner was assailed with even more ridicule when he exposed his works to the British public. What would have happened to Turner if Ruskin had not arisen to be his prophet I do not know. His pictures might not even have been moldering in the cellars of the National Gallery. They might have been selling at little second-hand shops in back streets for ten shillings to any one who had eyes in his head. Wordsworth, Browning, and Turner were all people of such original and unprecedented genius that there was no taste and interest for them when they appeared; they had to create the very power of understanding themselves. A poet of less original genius, a great genius but less of a genius, like Tennyson, comes along, and he writes about the "May Queen" and "The Northern Farmer," and all those simple, elementary things which immediately fetch the handkerchiefs out. Now no doubt to do that properly takes a certain amount of genius. But it taps the prompt and fluent emotions; and the misfortune is that kind of work is easily counterfeited and abused by those who wish to exploit our feelings rather than exalt them. It is a more easy kind of thing than was done by those great geniuses I first named. Original poets like Wordsworth and Browning had to create the taste for their work.

Now in like manner Christ had to make the soul which should respond to Him and understand Him. He had to create the very capacity for response. And that is where we are compelled to recognize the doctrine of the Holy Spirit as well as the doctrine of the Savour. We are always told that faith is the gift of God and the work of the Holy Spirit. The reason why we are told that, and must be told it, lies in the direction I have indicated. The death of Christ had not simply to touch like heroism, but it had to redeem us into power of feeling its own worth. Christ had to save us from what we were too far gone to feel. Just as the man choked with damp in a mine, or a man going to sleep in arctic cold, does not realize his danger, and the sense of danger has to be created within him, so the violent action of the Spirit takes men by force. The death of Christ must call up more than a responsive feeling. It is not satisfied with affecting our heart. That is mere impressionism. It is very easy to impress an audience. Every preacher knows that there is nothing more simple than to produce tears. You have only to tell a certain number of stories about dying children, lifeboats, fire escapes, and so on, and you can make people thrill. But the thrill is neither here nor there. What is the thrill going to end in? What is the meaning of the thrill for life? If it is not ending as it should, and not ending for life, it is doing harm, not good, because it is sealing the springs of feeling and searing the power of the spiritual life.

What the work of Christ requires is the tribute not of our admiration or even gratitude, not of our impressions or our thrills, but of ourselves and our shame. Now we are coming to the crux of the matter - the tribute of our shame. That death had to make new men of us. It had to turn us not from potential friends to actual, but from enemies into friends. It had not merely to touch a spring of slumbering friendship. There was a new creation. The love of God - I quote Paul, who did understand something of these things - the love of God is not merely evoked within us, it is "shed abroad in our hearts by the Holy Spirit which is given to us." That is a very different thing from simply having the reservoir of natural feeling tapped. The death of Christ had to do with our sin and not with our sluggishness. It had to deal with our active hostility, and not simply with the passive dullness of our hearts.

Our hostility - that is what the easy-going people cannot be brought to recognize. That is what the shallow optimists, who think we can now dispense with emphasis on the death of Christ, feel themselves able to do - to ignore the fact that the human heart is enmity against God, against a God who makes demands upon it; who goes so far as to make demands for the whole, the absolute obedience of self. Human nature puts its back up against that. That is what Paul means when he speaks about human nature, the natural man - the carnal man is a bad translation - being enmity against God. Man will cling to the last rag of his self-respect. He does not part with that when he thrills, admires, sympathizes; but he does when he has to give up his whole self in the obedience of faith. How much self-respect do you think Paul had left in him when he went into Damascus? Christ, with the demand for saving obedience, arouses antagonism in the human heart. And so will the Church that is faithful to Him. You hear people of the type I have been speaking about saying, If only the Church had been true to Christ's message it would have done wonders for the world. If only Christ were preached and practiced in all His simplicity to the world, how fast Christianity would spread. Would it? Do you really find that the deeper you get into Christ and the meaning of His demands Christianity spreads faster in your heart? Is it not very much the other way? When it comes to close quarters you have actually to be got down and broken, that the old man may be pulverized and the new man created from the dust. Therefore when we hear people abusing the Church and its history the first thing we have to say is, Yes, there is a great deal too much truth in what you say, but there is also a greater truth which you are not allowing for, and it is this. One reason why the Church has been so slow in its progress in mankind and its effect on human history is because it has been so faithful to Christ, so faithful to His Cross. You have to subdue the most intractable, difficult, and slow thing in the world - man's self-will. You cannot expect rapid successes if you truly preach the Cross whereon Christ died, and which He surmounted not simply by leaving it behind but by rising again, and converting the very Cross into a power and glory.

Christ arouses antagonism in the human heart and heroism does not. Everybody welcomes a hero. The minority welcome Christ. We do resent His absolute command. We do resent parting completely with ourselves. We do resent Christ.

4. I go back to the word I spoke about the tribute of our shame. The demand is unsparing, remorseless. It is not simply that you are called on by God for a certain due, a change, an amendment, but for the tribute of yourself and your shame. When you heard about that heroism of my story, when you thrilled to it, I wonder did you pat yourself on the back a little for being capable of thrilling to things so high, so fine? When you thrilled to that story you felt a certain satisfaction with yourself because there was as much of the God in you as allowed you to be capable of thrilling to such heroisms. You felt, If I am capable of thrilling to such things, I cannot be such a bad sort. But when you felt the meaning of Christ's death for you, did you ever pat yourself on the back? The nearer the Cross came to you, the deeper it entered into you, were you the more disposed to admire yourself? There is no harm in your feeling pleased with yourself because you were able to thrill to these

human heroisms; but if the impression Christ makes upon you is to leave you more satisfied with yourself, more proud of yourself for being able to respond, He has to get a great deal nearer to you yet. You need to be - I will use a Scottish phrase which old ministers used to apply to a young minister when he had preached a "thoughtful and interesting discourse" - you need to be well shaken over the mouth of the pit. The great deep classic cases of Christian experience bear testimony to that. Christ and His Cross come nearer and nearer, and we do not realize what we owe Him until we realize that He has plucked us from the fearful pit, and the miry clay, and set us upon a rock of God's own founding. The meaning of Christ's death rouses our shame, self-contempt, and repentance. And we resent being made to feel ashamed of ourselves, we resent being made to feel ashamed of ourselves, we resent being made to repent. A great many people are afraid to come too near to anything that does that for them. That is a frequent reason for not going to church.

5. Again, continuing. You would have gone a long way to see this Belgian man. You would have gazed upon him with something of reverence, certainly with admiration. You would have regarded him as one received back from the dead. You think, If all men were like that, the world would be heaven. Well, there are a great many more like that than we think, who daily imperil their life for their duty. But supposing every man and woman in the world were up to that pitch, and supposing you added them all together and took the total value of their moral heroism (if moral quantities were capable of being summed like that), would you then have the equivalent of the deed and death of Christ? No, indeed! If you took all the world, and made heroes of them all, and kept them heroic all their lives, instead of only in one act, still you would not get the value, the equivalent, of Christ's sacrifice. It is not the sum of all heroisms. It would be more true to say it is the source of all heroisms, the foundation of them all. It is the underground something that makes heroisms, not something that heroisms make up. When Christ did what He did, it was not human nature doing it, it was God doing it. That is the great, absolutely unique and glorious thing. It is God in Christ reconciling. It was not human nature offering its very best to God. It was God offering His very best to man. That is the grand difference between the Church and civilization, even when civilization is religious. We must attend more to those great issues between our faith and our world. Our religion has been too much a thing done in a corner. We must adjust our religion to the great currents and movements of the world's history. And the great issue of the hour is the issue between the Church and civilization. Their essential difference is this. Civilization at its best represents the most man can do with the world and with human nature; but the Church, centered upon Christ, His Cross, and His work, represents the best that God can do upon them. The sacrifice of the Cross was not man in Christ pleasing God; it was God in Christ reconciling man, and in a certain sense, reconciling Himself. My point at this moment is that the Cross of Christ was Christ reconciling man. It was not heroic man dying for a beloved and honored God; it was God in some form dying for man. God dying for man. I am afraid of that phrase; I cannot do without it. God dying for man; and for such men -hostile, malignantly hostile men. That is a puzzling phrase where we read

in a gospel: "Greater love hath no man that this, that a man lay down his life for his friends." There is more love in the phrase of the epistle, that a man should lay down his life for his bitter enemies. It is not so heroic, so very divine, to die for our friends. Kindness between the nice people is not so very divine - fine and precious as it is. To die for enemies - that is the divine thing. Christ's was grace that died for such for malignant enemies. There is more in God than love. There is all that we mean by His holy grace. Truly, "God is love." Yes, but the kind of love which you must interpret by the whole of the New Testament. When John said that, did he mean that God was simply the consummation of human affection? He knew that he was dealing with a holy, gracious God, a God who loved His enemies and redeemed them. Read with extreme care 1 John 4:10.

6. Let me gather up the points of difference which I have been indication.

First, that Belgian hero did not act from love so much as from duty. Secondly, he died only in one act, not in his whole life, dying daily. There have been men capable of acts of sacrifice like this hero; loose-living men who, after a heroism, were quite capable of returning to their looseness of life - heroes of the Bret Harte type. There have been many valiant, fearless things done on the battlefield by men who in the face of bullets never flinched, never turned a hair; and when they came home they could not stand against a breath of ridicule, they could not stand against a little temptation, and were soon wallowing in the mire. One act of sacrifice is not the same thing as a life gathered into one consummate sacrifice, whose value is that it has the whole personality put into it for ever.

Third, this man could not take the full measure of all that he was doing, and Christ could. Christ did not go to His death with His eyes shut. He died because He willed to die, having counted the cost with the greatest, deepest moral vision in the world.

Fourthly, the hero in the story had nothing to do with the moral condition of those whom he saved. The scoundrel and the saint in that train were both alike to him.

Again, he had no quarrel with those whom he saved. He had nothing to complain of. He had nothing from them to try his heroism. They were not his bitter enemies. His valour was not the heroism of forgiveness, where lies the wondrous majesty of God. His act was not an act of grace, which is the grand glory of the love of Christ. Christ died for people who not only did not know Him, but who hated and despised Him. He died, not for a trainful of people, but for the whole organic world of people. It was an infinite death, that of His, in its range and in its power. It was death for enemies more bitter than anything that man can feel against man, for such haters as only holiness can produce. Here is the singular thing: the greater the favour that is done to us, the more fiercely we resent it if it does not break us down and make us grateful. The greater the favour, if we do not respond in its own spirit, so much the more resentful and antagonistic it makes us. I have already said that we speak too often as though the effect of Christ's death upon human nature must be gratitude as soon as it is understood. It is not always gratitude. Unless it is received in the Holy Ghost, the effect may just be the other way. It is judgment. It is a death unto death.

I conclude by saying what I have often said, and what often needs saying, that it is not possible to hear the gospel and to go away just as you came. I wish that were more realized. We should not have so many sermon-hunters. If people felt that every time they heard the gospel they were either better or worse for it, they would be more careful about hearing. They would not go so often, possibly; better they should not perhaps. I am not speaking about hearing of sermons. That is neither here nor there. A man may hear sermons and be neither the better nor the worse. But a man cannot hear the gospel without being either better or worse, whether he knows it or not. When you come to face the last issues, it is either unto salvation or unto condemnation. The great central, decisive thing, the last judgment of the world, is the Cross of Christ. The reason why so many sermons are found uninteresting is not always due to the dullness of the preacher. God knows how often that is the case, but it is not always. It is because the sermons so often turn, or ought to turn, upon the miracle of the grace of God, which is so great a miracle that it is strange, remote, and alien to our natural ways of thinking and feeling. It seems foreign to us. It is like reading a guide-book if you have never been in the country. I take down my Baedeker in the winter and read it with the greatest delight, because I know the country. If I had not been there I should find it the dreariest reading. Why do not people read the Bible more? Because they have not been in that country. There is no experience for it to stir and develop. The Cross of Christ, the infinite wonder of it - we have got to learn that. We have got to learn the deep meaning of that by having been there, by the evangelical experience whose lack is the cause of all the religious vagrancy of the hour. We have got to learn that it was not simply magnificent heroism, but that it was God in Christ reconciling the world. It was God that did that work in Christ. And Christ was the living God working upon man, and working out the Kingdom of God.

II. The Great Sacrificial Work Is To Reconcile

Corinthians 5:14-6:2; Romans 5:1-11; Colossians 1:10-29; Ephesians 2:16

The great need of the religious world today is a return to the Bible. That is necessary for two reasons, negative and positive. Negatively, because the most serious feature of the hour in the life of the Church is the neglect of the Bible for personal use and study by religious people. Positively, because we have today enormous advantages in connection with that return to the Bible. Modern scholarship has made of the Bible a new Book. It has in a certain sense rediscovered it. You might say that the soul of the Reformation was the rediscovery of the Bible; and in a wider sense that is true today also. We have, through the labors of more than a century of the finest scholarship in all the world, come to understand the Bible, in its original sense, as it was never understood before. These instructed scribes draw forth from their treasury things as new as old. It is the old Book, and it is a new Book. It is the old Book, and the precious Book, because of its power of unceasing self-renovation. The spirit that lives within the Bible is a spirit of constant self-preservation. One way of describing the Reformation is to say that, since the early Gnostic centuries, it was the greatest effort that ever took place in the Church for the self-preservation of Christianity. Remember, the Church was not reformed from the outside, but from the inside. It was the Church reforming the Church. It was the Church's faith that arose, under the Holy Spirit, and reformed the Church. So it is with the Bible. Whatever renovation we find in connection with the Bible - I do not here man renovation of ourselves, but renovation of our way of understanding the Book - arises out of the Bible itself. This remains true today, as it was true in the Reformation time, although it is now true in a somewhat different application. The Bible is still the best commentary upon itself. I have always done much in my ministry in the way of expounding the Bible, and I would say to the younger ministers particularly who are here, Do not be afraid of that manner of preaching. I have known young ministers who were over-scrupulous I have known them say, "If I take a long text people will think it is because I am lazy and do not want the labour of getting a sermon out of a small one." Never mind such foolish people. Do not be afraid of long texts, long passages. Preach less from verses and more from paragraphs. If I had my time over again I would do a great deal more in that way than I have done. Read but one lesson, and read it with elucidatory comments. Of course some people can do that better than others. There is always the danger that if a person try it who has no sort of knack in that direction, the people will feel they have been let in for two sermons instead of one; and, excellent as these might be, people do not like to feel they have been got to church upon false pretenses. It might even given an excuse to certain people for omitting one of the services altogether, on the plea they had put in the requisite amount of attention at one service. I would also admit that if you do this it will not reduce your labour. It will really add what might amount to another sermon to your weekly work. It is no use doing it if you do it on the spur of the moment. If you just say things that occur to your mind while you are reading, you may say some banal, or some nonsensical and fantastic things. It means careful preparation. The lesson should be prepared as truly as the prayer should be prepared, and as the sermon should be prepared. You have to work your way through the chapter with the aid of the best commentary that you can get; and you have to exercise continual judgment in doing so lest you be dragged away into little matters of detail instead of keeping to the larger lines of thought in the passage in hand. Then, if you do as I say, there is this other advantage, that you can take a particular verse out of the long passage for your sermon; and thus you come to the sermon with an audience which you yourself have prepared to listen to you. You have created your own atmosphere, and you have done it on a Bible basis.

Now I will confess against myself that sometimes, as I preach about here and there, and have done as I have been recommending you to do, people have come to me afterwards and said, as nicely as they could, that the sermon was all very well, but in respect of the reading of the Scripture, they never heard it after that fashion; they had never realized how vivid Scripture could become. That simply results from paying attention to the chapter with the best help. You will find, I am sure, that your congregation will welcome it.

Supposing, then, we return to the Bible. Supposing that the Church did - as I think it must do if it is not going to collapse; certainly the Free Churches must - supposing we return to the Bible, there are three ways of reading the Bible. The first way asks, What did the Bible say? The second way asks, What can I make the Bible say? The third way asks, What does God say in the Bible?

The first way is, with the aid of these magnificent scholars, to discover the true historic sense of the Bible. There is no more signal illustration of success here than in the case of the Prophets. During the time when theology dominated everything and was considered to be the Church's one grand concern, about one hundred years after the Reformation, when its great prophets had passed away, and the Church had fallen into different hands, the whole of the Old Testament - the Prophets amongst the rest - was read for proof passages of theological doctrines. Now for books like the Prophets that is absolutely fatal - fatal to the books and to the Church; and fatal in the long run to Christian truth. There is no greater service that has been done to the Bible than what has been done by the scholars I speak of, in making the Prophets live again, putting them in their true historical setting and position. Dr. George Adam Smith, for example, has done inestimable service in this way. And what has been done for the Prophets has also been done for the New Testament. Immense steps onward have been taken; and we are coming to know with much exactness what the writer actually had in his mind at the moment of writing, and what he was understood to have had in his mind by those to whom he first wrote. In this way we get rid, for example, of the idea that Paul was thinking about us who live two thousand years after him. He was not thinking of us at all. He did not expect the world to last a century. It is quite another question what the Holy Spirit was thinking about. Paul was thinking in a natural way about his age and his Churches, about their actual situation and needs. That is another illustration of the principle that if you want to work for immortality you must work in the most relevant and faithful way amid the circumstances round about you. The present duty is the path to immortality. And so also I might illustrate in respect to the Gospels.

The second way of reading the Bible is reading it unto edification. That is to say, we read a passage, and we allow ourselves to receive any suggestion that may come to us from it, and we do not stop to ask whether that was in the writer's mind, or whether it was in the mind of the people to whom he wrote. That is immaterial. We allow the Spirit of God to suggest to us whatever lessons or ideas He thinks fit out of the words that are under our eyes. We read the Bible not for correct or historic knowledge, but for religious and spiritual purposes, for our own private and personal needs. That is, or course, a perfectly legitimate thing - indeed, it is quite necessary. It is the way of reading the Bible which the large mass of the Church must always practice. But it has its dangers. You need the other ways to correct it. All the three must cooperate for the true use and understanding of the Bible by the Church at large. But I am speaking now about its use by individuals, and the danger I mean is that the suggestiveness may sometimes become fantastic. Some preachers fail at times in that way. They get to taking what are called fancy texts, texts which impress the audience much more with the ingenuity of the preacher than with his inspiration. For instance, a preacher in the North, now dead, was preaching against the Higher Criticism and its slicing up of the Bible, and he took his text from Nehemiah, "He cut it with a penknife"! That is all very well, perhaps, for a motto, but for a text it is rather a liberty. It is not fair to the Bible to indulge in much of that at least. If I remember rightly, Dr. Parker had a great gift in this way, and more than sometimes it ran way with him. It is a temptation of every witty man, and every ingenious-minded man. But there is a peril in it, the abuse of a right principle. We are bound, or course, to vindicate for ourselves and for others the right to use the Bible in the suggestive way, if we are not to make a present of it to the scholars. And that would be just as bad as making a present of it to a race of priests. But when we read too much in that way it is apt to become a minister to our spiritual egotism, or, what is equally bad, our fanciful subjectivity.

Now the grand value of the bible is just the other thing - its objectivity. The first thing is not how I feel, but it is, How does God feel, and what has God said or done for my soul? When we get to real close quarters with that our feeling and response will look after itself. Do not tell people how they ought to feel towards Christ. That is useless. It is just what they ought that they cannot do. Preach a Christ that will make them feel as they ought. That is objective preaching. The tendency and fashion of the present moment is all in the direction of subjectivity.

People welcome sermons of a more or less psychological kind, which go into the analysis of the soul or of society. They will listen gladly to sermons on character-building, for instance; and in the result they will get to think of nothing else but their own character. They will be the builders of their own character; which is a fatal thing. Learn to commit your soul and the building of it to One who can keep it and build it as you never can. Attend then to Christ, the Holy Spirit, the Kingdom, and the Cause, and He will look after your soul. A consequence of this passion for subjective and psychological analysis, for sentimental experience and problem-preaching a real, objective, New Testament gospel he has raised against him what is not the most fatal accusation - even within the Christian Church it has come to be very fatal - he is accused of being a theologian. That is a very fatal charge to make now against any preacher. It ought to be actionable in the way of libel. We have come to this - that if you penetrate into the interior of the New Testament you will be accused of being a theologian; and then it is all over with your welcome. But that state of things has to be turned upside down, else the Church dries into the sand. There is no message in it.

The third way of reading the Bible is reading it to discover the purpose and thought of God, whether it immediately edify us or whether it do not. If we did actually become aware of the will and thought of God it would edify us as nothing else could. No inner process, no discipline to which we might subject ourselves, no way of cultivating subjective holiness would do so much for us as if we could lose ourselves, and in some godly sort forget ourselves, because we are so preoccupied with the mind of Christ. If you want psychological analysis, analyze the will, work, and purpose of Christ our Lord. I read a fine sentence the other day which puts in a condensed form what I have often preached about as the symptom of the present age: "Instead of placing themselves at the service of God most people want a God who is at their service." These two tendencies represent in the end two different religions. The man who is exploiting God for the purposes of his own soul or for the race, has in the long run a different religion from the man who is putting his own soul and race absolutely at the disposal of the will of God in Jesus Christ.

All this is by way of preface to an attempt to approach the New Testament and endeavour to find what is really the will of God concerning Christ and what Christ did. Doctrine and life are really two sides of one Christianity; and they are equally indispensable, because Christianity is living truth. It is not merely truth; it is not simply life. It is living truth. The modern man says that doctrine which does not pass into life is dead; and then the mistake he makes is that he wants to turn it into life directly, and to politicize it, perhaps; whereas it works in-directly. The experience of many centuries, on the other hand, says that Christian life which does not grow out of Christian doctrine becomes a failure. If not in individuals, it does in the Church. You cannot keep Christian piety alive except upon Christian truth. You can never get a Catholic Church except by Catholic truth. I think perhaps we all here agree about that. It is of immense importance that we do not think entirely about our individual souls, and that we think more about the Church, the divine will, the divine Word, and the divine Kingdom in the world. It is of supreme importance that we should know what the Christian doctrine is on the great matters.

Now in connection with the work of Christ the great expositor in the Bible is St. Paul. And Paul has a word of his own to describe Christ's work - the word "reconciliation." But he thinks of reconciliation not as a doctrine but as an act of God - because he was not a theologian but an experience preacher. To view it so produces an immense change in your whole way of thinking. It secures for you all that is worth having in theology, and it delivers you from the danger of obsession by theology in a one-sided way. Remember, then, that the truth we are dealing with is precious not as a mere truth but as the means of expressing the eternal act of God. The most important thing in all the world, in the Bible or out of it, is something that God has done - for ever finally done. And it is this reconciliation; which is only secondarily a doctrine; it is only secondarily even a manner of life. Primarily it is an act of God. That is to say, it is a salvation before it is a religion. For Christianity as a religion stands upon salvation. Religion which does not grow out of salvation is not Christian religion; it may be spiritual, poetic, mystic; but the essence of Christianity is not just to be spiritual; it is to answer God's manner of spirituality, which you find in Jesus Christ and in Him crucified. Reconciliation is salvation before it is religion. And it is religion before it is theology. All our theology in this matter rests upon the certain experience of the fact of God's salvation. It is salvation upon divine principles It is salvation by a holy God. It is bound of course, to be theological in its very nature its statement is a theology. The moment you begin to talk about the holiness of God you are theologians. And you cannot talk about Christ and His death in any thorough way without talking about the holiness of God.

Christ and Him crucified, that is the historic fact. But what do I mean when I say Christ and Him crucified? Does it mean that a certain personality lived who was recognized in history as Jesus Christ, and that He came by His end by crucifixion? That in itself is worthless for religious purposes. It is useful enough if you are writing history; but for religion historical fact must have interpretation, and the whole of Christianity depends upon the interpretation that is put upon such facts. You will find people sometimes who say, "Let us have the simple historic facts, the Cross and Christ." That is not Christianity. Christianity is a certain interpretation of those facts. How and why did the New Testament come into being? Was it simply to convince posterity that those facts had taken place? Was it simply to convince the world that Christ had risen from the dead? If that were the grand object of the New Testament we should have a very different Bible in our hands, one addressed to the world and not to the Church, to critical science and not to faith; and there would not be so much argument amongst scholars as there is. The Bible did not come into being in order to provide future historians with a valuable document. It came for the purposes of interpretation. Here is a sentence I came across once: "The fact without the word is dumb; the word without the fact is empty." It is useful to turn it over and over in your mind.

Paul was almost the creator and the great representative of that interpretation. It was continued on his lines by Augustine, Anselm, Luther, and many another. But what is it that we hear about so much today? We hear a great deal about an undogmatic Christianity. And there is a certain plausibility in it. If you have no theological training, no training in the understanding of the Scripture in a serious way, that is, if you do not know your business as ministers of the Word, it seems natural that undogmatic Christianity should be just the thing you want. Leave the dogma of it, you will say, to those who devote their lives to dogma - just as though theologians were irrepressible people who take up theology as a hobby and become the bores of the Church! It was not a hobby to the apostles. Why, there are actually people of a similar stamp who look upon missions as a hobby of the Church, instead of their belonging to the very being and fidelity of the Church. So some people think theology is a hobby, and that theologians are persons with an uncomfortable preponderance of intellect, who are trying to destroy the privileges secured by our national lack of education and to sacrifice Christianity to mind. People say we do not want so much intellect in preaching; we want sympathy and unction. Now, I am always looking afield, and looking forward, and thinking about the prospects of the Church in the great world. And unction dissociated from Christian truth and Christian intelligence has at last the sentence of the Church's death within itself. You may cherish an undogmatic Christianity with a sort of magnetic casing, a purely human, mystical, subjective kind of Christ for yourself or an audience, but you could not continue to preach that in a Church for the ages. The Church could not live on that and do its preaching in such a world. You could not spread a gospel like that. Subjective religion is valuable in its place, but its place is limited. The only Cross you can preach to the whole world is a theological one. It is not the fact of the Cross, it is the interpretation of the Cross, the prime theology of the Cross, what God meant by the Cross, that is everything. That is what the New Testament came to give. That is the only kind of Cross that can make or keep a Church.

You will say, perhaps, "Cannot I go out and preach my impressions of the Cross?" By all means. You will only discover the sooner that you cannot preach a Cross to any purpose if you preach it only as an experience. If you only preach it so you would not be an apostle; and you could not do the work of an apostle for the Church The apostles were particular about this, and one expressed it quite pointedly: "We preach not ourselves [not our experiences] but Christ crucified." "We do not preach religion," said Paul, "but God's revelation. We do not preach the impression the Cross made upon us, but the message that God by His Spirit sent through a Christ we experience." And so with ourselves. We do not preach our impressions, or even our experience. These make but the vehicle, as it were. What we preach is something much more solid, more objective, with more stay in it; something that can suffice when our experience has ebbed until it seems to be as low as Christ's was in the great desertion and victory on the Cross. We want something that will stand by us when we cannot feel any more; we want a Cross we can cling to, not simply a subjective Cross. That is, to put the thing in another way, what we want today is an insight into the Cross. You see I am making a distinction between impression and insight. It is a useful part of the Church's work, for instance, that it should act by means of revival services, where perhaps the dominant element may be temporary impression. But unless that is taken up and turned to account by something more, we all know how evanescent a thing it is apt to be. We need, not simply to be impressed by Christ, but to see into Christ and into His Cross. We need to deepen the impression until it become new life by seeing into Christ. There are certain circumstances in which we may be entitled to declare that we do not want so many people who glibly say they love Jesus; we want more people who can really see into Christ. We do, of course, want more people who love Jesus; but we want a multitude of more people who are not satisfied with that, but whose love fills them with holy curiosity and compels them habitually to cultivate in the Spirit the power of seeing into Christ and into His Cross. More than impression, do we need a spirit of divination. Insight is what we want for power - less of mere interest and more of real insight. There are some people who talk as though, when we speak of the Cross and the meaning of the Cross, we were spinning something out of the Cross. Paul was not spinning anything out of the Cross. He was gazing into the Cross, seeing what was really there with eyes that had been unsealed and purged by the Holy Ghost.

The doctrine of Christ's reconciliation, or His Atonement, is not a piece of mediaeval dogma like transubstantiation, not a piece of ecclesiastical dogma or Aristotelian subtlety which it might be the Bible's business to destroy. If you look at the Gospels you will see that from the Transfiguration onward this matter of the Cross is the great center of concern; it is where the center of gravity lies. I met a man the other day who had come under some poor and mischievous pulpit influence, and he said, "It is time we got rid of hearing so much about the Cross of Christ; there should be preached to the world a humanitarian Christ, the kind of Christ that occupies the Gospels." There was nothing for it but to tell that man he was the victim of smatterers, and that he must go back to his Gospels and read and study for a year or two. It is the flimsiest religiosity, and the most superficial reading of the Gospel, that could talk like that. What does it mean that an enormous proportion of the Gospel story is occupied with the passion of Christ? The center of gravity, even in the Gospels, falls upon the Cross of Christ and what was done there, and not simply upon a humanitarian Christ. You cannot set the Gospels against Paul. Why, the first three Gospels were much later than Paul's Epistles. They were written for Churches that were made by the apostolic preaching. But how, then, do the first three Gospels *seem* so different from the Epistles? If course, there is a superficial difference. Christ was a very living and real character for the people of His own time, and His grand business was to rouse his audiences' faith in His Person and in His mission. But in His Person and in His mission the Cross lay latent all the time. It emerged only in the fullness of time - that valuable phrase - just when the historic crisis, the organic situation, produced it. Jesus was not a professor of theology. He did not lecture the people. He did not come with a theology of the Cross. He did not come to force events to comply with that theology. He did not force His own people to work out a theological scheme. He did force an issue, but it was not to illustrate a theology. It was to establish the Kingdom of God, which could be established in no other wise than as He established it - upon the Cross. And He could only teach the Cross when it had happened - which He did through the Evangelists with the space they gave it, and through the Apostles and the exposition they gave it.

To come back to this work of Christ described by Paul as reconciliation. On this interpretation of the work of Christ the whole Church rests. If you move faith from that enter you have driven *the* nail into the Church's coffin. The Church is then doomed to death, and is only a matter of time when she shall expire. The Apostle, I say, described the work of Christ as above all things reconciliation. And Paul was the founder of the Church, historically speaking. I do not like to speak of Christ as the Founder of the Church. It seems remote, detached, journalistic. It would be far more true to say that He is the foundation of the Church. "The Church's one foundation is Jesus Christ her Lord." The founder of the Church, historically speaking, was Paul. It was founded by and through him on this reconciling principle - may, I go deeper than that, on this mighty *act* of God's reconciliation. For this great act the interpretation was given to Paul by the Holy Spirit. In this connection read that great word in 1 Corinthians 2; that is the most valuable word in the New Testament about the nature of apostolic inspiration.

What, then, did Paul mean by this reconciliation which is the backbone of the Church? He meant the total result of Christ's life-work in permanently changing the relation between collective man and God. By reconciliation Paul meant the total result of Christ's life-work in the fundamental, permanent, final changing of the relation between man and God, altering it from a relation of hostility to one of confidence and peace. Remember, I am speaking as Paul spoke, about man, and not about individual men or groups of men.

There are two principal Greek words connected with the idea of reconciliation, one of them being always translated by it, the other sometimes. They are *katallassein,* and *hilaskesthai* - reconciliation and atonement. Atonement is an Old Testament phrase, where the idea is that of the covering of sin from God's sight. But by whom? Who was that great benefactor of the human race that succeeded in covering up our sin from God's sight? Who was skillful enough to hoodwink the Almighty? Who covered the sin? The all-seeing God alone. There can therefore be no talk of hoodwinking. Atonement means the covering of sin by something which God Himself had provided, and therefore the covering of sin by God Himself. It was of course not the blinding of Himself to it, but something very different. How could the Judge of all the earth make His judgment blind? It was the covering of sin by something which makes it lose the power of deranging the covenant relation between God and man and founds the new Humanity. That is the meaning of it.

If you think I am talking theology, you must blame the New Testament. I am simply expounding to you the New Testament. Of course, you need not take it unless you please. It is quite open to you to throw the New Testament overboard (so long as you are frank about it), and start what you may loosely call Christianity on the floating lines. But if you take the New Testament you are bound to try to understand the New Testament. If you understand the New Testament you are bound to recognize that this is what the New Testament says. It is a subsequent question whether the New Testament is right in saying so. Let us first find out what the Bible really says, and then discuss whether the Bible is right or wrong.

The idea of atonement is the covering of sin by something which God provided, and by the use of which sin looses its accusing power, and its power to derange that grand covenant and relationship between man and God which founds the New Humanity. The word *katallassein* (reconcile) is peculiar to Paul. He uses both words; but the other word, "atonement," you also find in other New Testament writings. Reconciliation is Paul's great characteristic word and thought. The great passages are those I have mentioned at the head of this lecture. I cannot take time to expound them here. That would mean a long course. Read those passages carefully and check me in anything I say - particularly, fir instance, 2 Corinthians 5:15 - 6:2. Out of it we gather this whole result. First, Christ's work is something described as reconciliation. And second, reconciliation rests upon atonement as its ground. Do not stop at "God was in Christ reconciling the world." You can easily water that down. You may begin the process by saying that God was in Christ just in the same way in which He was in the old prophets. That is the first dilution. Then you go on with the homeopathic treatment, and you say, "Oh yes, all He did by Christ was to affect the world, and impress it by showing it how much He loved it." Now would that reconcile anybody really in need of it? When your child has flown into a violent temper with you, and still worse, a sulky temper, and glooms for a whole day, is it any use your sending to that child and saying, "Really, this cannot go on. Come back. I love you very much. Say you are sorry." Not a bit of use. For God simply to have told or shown the evil world how much He loved it would have been a most ineffectual thing. Something had to be *done* - judging or saving. Revelation alone is inadequate. Reconciliation must rest on atonement. For, as I say, you must not stop at "God was in Christ reconciling the world unto Himself," but go on "not reckoning unto them their trespasses." "He made Christ to be sin for us, who knew no sin." that involves atonement. You cannot blot out that phrase. And the third thing involved in the idea is that this reconciliation, this atonement, means change of relation between God and man - man, mind you, not two or three men, not several groups of men, but man, the human race as one whole. And it is a change of relation from alienation to communion - not simply to our peace and confidence, but to reciprocal communion. The grand end of reconciliation is communion. I am pressing that hard. I am pressing it hard here by saying that it is not enough that we should worship God. It is not enough that we should worship a personal God. It is not enough that we should worship and pay our homage to a loving God. That does not satisfy the love of God. Nothing short of living, loving, holy habitual communion between His holy soul and ours can realize at last the end which God achieved in Jesus Christ.

In this connection let me offer you two cautions. First, take care that the direct fact of reconciliation is not hidden up by the indispensable means - namely, atonement. There have been ages in the Church when the attention has been so exclusively centered upon atonement that reconciliation was lost sight of. You found theologians flying at each other's throats in the interest of particular theories of atonement. That is to say, atonement had obscured reconciliation. In the same way, after the Reformation period, they dwelt upon justification until they lost sight of sanctification altogether. Then the great pietistic movement had to arise in order to redress the balance. Take care that the end, reconciliation, is not hidden up by the means, atonement. Justification, sanctification, reconciliation and atonement are all equally inseparable from the one central and compendious work of Christ. Various ages need various aspects of it turned outward. Let us give them all their true value and perspective. If we do not we shall make that fatal severance which orthodoxy has so often made between doctrine and life.

The second caution is this. Beware of reading atonement out of reconciliation altogether. Beware of cultivating a reconciliation which is not based upon justification. The apostle's phrases are often treated like that. They are emptied of the specific Christian meaning. There are a great many Christian people, spiritual people of a sort, today, who are perpetrating that injustice upon the New Testament. They are taking mighty old words and giving them only a subjective, arbitrary meaning, emptying out of them the essential, objective, positive content. They are preoccupied with what takes place within their own experience, or imagination, or thought; and they are oblivious of that which is declared to have taken place within the experience of God and of Christ. They are oblivious and negligent of the essential things that Christ did, and God in Christ. That is not fair treatment of New Testament terms - to empty them of positive Christian meaning and water them down to make something that might suit a philosophic or mystic or subjective or individualist spirituality. There is a whole system of philosophy that has attempted this dilution at the present day. It is associated with a name that has now become very well known, the name of the greatest philosopher the world ever saw, Hegel. I am not now going to expound Hegelianism. But I have to allude to one aspect of it. If you are paying any attention to what is going on around you in the thinking world, you are bound to come face to face with some phase of it or other. But I see my time is at an end for today.

Tomorrow I begin where I now leave off and shall say something about this version of St. Paul's idea of reconciliation, which is so attractive philosophically. I remember the appeal it had for me when I came into contact with it first. I did feel that it seemed to give a largeness to certain New Testament terms, which I finally found was a largeness of latitude only. If it did seem to give breadth it did not give depth. And I close here by reminding you of this - that while Christ and Christianity did come to make us broad men, it did not come to do that in the first instance. It came to make us deep men. The living interest of Christ and of the Holy Spirit is not breadth, but it is depth. Christ said little that was wide compared with what He said piercing and searching. I illustrate by referring you to an interest that is very prominent amongst you - the interest of missions. How did modern missions arise? I mean the last hundred years of them. Modern Protestant missions are only one hundred years old. Where did they begin? Who began them? They began at the close of the eighteenth century, the century whose close was dominated by philosophers, by scientists, by a reasonable, moderate interpretation of religion, by broad humanitarian religion. Of course, you might expect it was amongst those broad people that missions arose. We know better. We know that the Christian movement which has spread around the world did not arise out of the liberal thinkers, the humanitarian philosophers of the day, who were its worst enemies, but with a few men - Carey, Marshman, Ward, and the like - whose Calvinistic theology we should now consider very narrow. But they did have the root of the universal matter in them. A gospel deep enough has all the breadth of the world in its heart. If we are only deep enough the breadth will take care of itself. I would ten times rather have one man who was burning deep, even though he wanted to burn me for my modern theology, than I would have a broad, hospitable, and thin theologian who was willing to take me in and a nondescript crowd of others in a sheet let down from heaven, but who had no depth, no fire, no skill to search, and no power to break. For the deep Christianity is that which not only searches us, but breaks us. and a Christianity which would exclude none has no power to include the world.

III. Reconciliation: Philosophic and Christian

I place on the board before you five points as to Christ's reconciling work which I think vital:
1. It is between person and person. 2. Therefore it affects both sides. 3. It rest on atonement. 4. It is a reconciliation of the world as one whole. 5. It is final in its nature and effect.

I was saying yesterday that two cautions ought to be observed in connection with this matter of reconciliation. First, we should not hide up the idea of reconciliation by the idea of atonement; we should not obscure the end, or the effect, by the great and indispensable means to it. Second, at the other extreme we are to beware of emptying reconciliation of atonement altogether. Two very great thinkers arose last century in Germany - where most of the thinking on this subject has for the last hundred years been done. Much of our work has been to steal. That does not matter if it is done wisely and gratefully. When a man gives out a great thought, get it, work it; it is common property. It belongs to the whole world, to be claimed and assimilated by whoever shall find. Well, there were two very powerful men in Germany much opposed to each other, yet at a certain point at one - Hegel and Ritschl. While they preached the doctrine of reconciliation in different senses, they both united to obscure the idea of atonement or expiation. Now we are to beware of emptying the reconciliation idea of the idea of atonement, whether we do it philosophically with Hegel or theologically with Ritschl. I mention these men because their thought has very profoundly affected English thinking, whether philosophical or theological. I protested yesterday against the practice, so common, of taking New Testament words, and words consecrated to Christian experience, emptying them of their essential content, and keeping them in a vapid use. That is done for various reasons. It is sometimes done because the words are too valuable to be parted with; sometimes because a philosophic interpretation seems to rescue them from the narrowness of an outworn theology; and it is sometimes done for lower motives in order to produce a fictitious impression upon people that they are still substantially hearing the substance of the old truths when really they are not.

Especially I began yesterday to call attention to the view which is associated with the philosophical position of Hegel. Being a philosopher he was great upon the idea. The whole world, he said, was a movement or process of the grand, divine idea; but it was a *process*. Now please to put down and make much use of this fundamental distinction between a process and an act. A process had nothing moral in it. We are simply carried along on the crest of a wave. An act, on the other hand, can only be done by a moral personality. The act involves the notion of will and responsibility, and, indeed, the whole existence of a moral world. The process destroys that notion. Now the general tendency of philosophy is to devote itself to the idea and to the process. Science, for example, which is the ground floor, not to say the basement, of philosophy - science knows nothing about acts, it only knows about processes. The chemist knows only about processes. The biologist knows only about processes. The psychologist treats even acts as processes. But the theologian, and, indeed, religion altogether, stands or falls with the idea of an act. For him an infinite process is at bottom an eternal act. The philosophical thinker says the world is the process of an evolving idea, which may be treated as personal or may not. But for Christianity the world is the action of the eternal, divine act, a moral act, an act of will and of conscience.

Let us see how this applies to our thoughts about reconciliation. I have already indicated to you that the grand goal of the divine reconciliation is communion with God, not simply that we should be in tune with the Infinite, as an attractive but thin book has it. The object of the divine atonement is something much more than bringing us into time with God. It is more than raising our pitch and defining our note. It means that we are brought into actual, reciprocal communion with God out of guilt. We have personal intercourse with the Holy, we exchange thoughts and feelings. But this Christian idea of reconciliation, the idea of communion with the living and holy God, is replaced in philosophic theology by another idea, that, namely, of adjustment to rational Godhead, our adjustment to that mighty idea, that mighty rational process, which is moving on throughout the world. Sometimes the Godhead is conceived as personal, sometimes as impersonal; but in any case reconciliation would be rather a resigned adjustment to this great and overwhelming idea, which, having issued everything, is perpetually recalling, or exalting, everything into fusion with itself. But fusion, however organic and concrete, is one thing, communion is another thing. An individual might be lost in the great sum of being as a drop of water is lost in the ocean. That is fusion. Or it might be taken up as a cell in the body's organic process. That is a certain kind of reconciliation or absorption. But moral, spiritual reconciliation, where we have personal beings to deal with, is much more than fusion; more than absorption; it is communion. It is more than placing us in our niche. When we think in the philosophic way it practically means that reconciliation is understood almost entirely from man's side, without realizing the divine initiative as an act. But such divine initiative is everything. It is in the mercy of our God that all our hopes begin. Nothing that confuses that gets at the root of our Christian reconciliation. Or, sometimes, those philosophic ideas are carried so far that God's concern for the individual is ignored. These great processes work according to general laws; and general laws, like Acts of Parliament, are bound to do some injustice to individuals. You cannot possibly get complete justice by Act of Parliament. It is bound to hit somebody very hard. And it has often been doubted by exponents of philosophical theology such as I describe whether the individual as an individual was really present to God's mind and affection at all. And they think prayer is unreasonable except for its reflex effect on us. Thus the whole stress comes to be put upon our attitude to God, and not upon a reciprocal relationship. That is to say, religion becomes, as I described yesterday, a subjectivity, a resignation. In others it becomes a sense of dependence. People are invited to become preoccupied with their own attitude, their own relation, their own feelings toward the unchangeable, but absorbing, and even unfeeling God. Attention is directed upon the human side instead of insight cultivated into the divine side. The result of that practically is that religion comes to consist far too much in working up a certain frame of feeling instead of dwelling upon the objective reality of the act of God. Resignation is, then, my act; but it is not resignation to a sympathetic act of approach in God, but only to His onward movement. But, as I have said before, if we are to produce the real Christian faith we must dwell upon, we must preach and press, that objective act and gift of God which in itself produces that faith. We cannot produce it. Many try. There are some people who actually work at holiness. It is a dangerous thing to do, to work at your own holiness. The way to cultivate the holiness of the New Testament is to cultivate the New Testament Christ, the interpretation of Christ in His Cross, by His Spirit, which cannot but produce holiness, and holiness of a far profounder order than anything we may make by taking ourselves to pieces and putting ourselves together in the best way we can, or by adjusting ourselves with huge effort to a universal process. Religious subjectivity is truly a most valuable phase; and at some periods in the Church's history it is urgently called for. In the seventeenth century it was so called for because Protestantism had degenerated into a mere theological orthodoxy, a very hard-shell kind of Christianity. It was necessary that the great Pietistic movement should arise and correct it. But this is itself a danger in turn; and we have to rise up in the name of the gospel, of the New Testament, and demand a more objective religion; and we have to declare that if ever divine holiness is to be produced in man it can only be produced by God's act through Christ in the Holy Spirit.

The philosophic kind of theology (which is rather theosophy) often ends, you perceive, in turning real reconciliation into something quite different. It becomes turned into the mere forced adjustment of man to his fate; and naturally this often ends in a resentful pessimism. Supposing the whole universe to be a vast rational process unfolding itself like an infinite cosmic flower, you cannot have communion or any hearty understanding between a living, loving soul and that evolutionary process. All you can do is to adjust yourself to that process, settle down to it and make the best of it, square yourself to it in the way that seems best for you, and that will cause you and others least discomfort. But reconciliation becomes debased indeed when it turns to mere resignation. Of course, we have to practice resignation. But Christianity is not the practice of resignation. At least, that is not the meaning of reconciliation. When two friends fall out and are reconciled, it does not simply mean that one adjusts himself to the other. That is a very one-sided arrangement. There must be a mutuality. Theology of the kind I have been describing has a great deal to say about men changing their way of looking at things or feeling about them. If I were preaching a theology like that I should say: "This mighty process, of which you are all parts, is unfolding itself to a grand closing result. It is going to be a grand thing for everybody in the long run (provided, that is, that they continue to exist as individuals and are capable of feeling anything, whether grand or mean). It is all going to work out to a grand consummation. You do not see that, but you must make an effort and accept it as the genius and drift of things; and that is faith. You must accept the idea that the whole world is working out, through much suffering and by many round-about ways, to a grand final consummation which will be a blessing for everybody, even though it might mean their individual extinction. What you have to do in these circumstances is, by a great act of faith, to believe that this is so and to immolate yourself, if need be, for the benefit of this grand whole; at any rate, accommodate yourself to its evolving movement."

The gospel of Christ speaks otherwise. It speaks of a God to whom we are to be reconciled in a mutual act which He begins; and not of an order or process with which we are to be adjusted by our lonely act, or to which we are to be resigned. If we have an idea of such a Godhead as I have been describing, how does it affect our thought of Christ? Christ then becomes but one of its grandest prophets, or one of the greatest instances and illustrations of that adjustment to the mighty order. He first realized, and He first declared, this great change in the way of reading the situation. What you have to do if you accept Him is to change your way of reading the situation, to accept His interpretation of life, and accept it as rationally, spiritually, and resignedly as you best can. Accept His principle. Die to live. But what a poor use of Christ - to accept His interpretation of life, as if He were a mere spiritual Goethe! That is a very attenuated Christ compared with the Christ that is offered to us in the New Testament. That is not the eternal Son of God in whom God was reconciling the world unto Himself. That is another Christ - from some hasty points of view indeed a larger Christ; for the philosophers have a larger Christ, apparently, one more cosmic. But it is a diluted Christ, and one that cannot penetrate to the center and depth of our human need or our human personality, cannot reach our guilt and hell, and therefore cannot be the final Christ of God.

Whether from the side of the philosophers, as I have been showing, or from the side of certain theologians like Ritschl, who was so much opposed to Hegel, you will often hear this said: that only man needed to be reconciled, that God did not need any reconciliation. Now, I have been asking you to observe that we are dealing with persons. That is the first point I put upon the board. Our reconciliation is between person and person. It is not between an order or a process on the one hand and a person on the other. Therefore a real and deep change of the relation between the two means a change on both sides. That is surely clear if we are dealing with living persons. God is an eternal person; I am a finite person; yet we are persons both. There is that parity. Any reconciliation which only means change on one side is not a real reconciliation at all. A real, deep change of relation affects both sides when we are dealing with persons. That is not the case when we are dealing on the one side with ideas, or one vast idea or process, and on the other side a person only.

When Christianity is being watered down in the way I have described, we have to concentrate our attention upon the core of it. All round us Christianity is being diluted either by thought or by *blague;* we must press to the core of the matter. It is true the theology of the Christian Church on this head needs a certain amount of modification and correction at the present day. That will appear presently. But I want to make it clear that the view of the Church upon the whole, especially the great view associated with the Reformation, preserves the core of the matter, which we are in danger of losing either on one side or the other.

Let me call your attention, then, to these five points, which you will find immanent in what I have subsequently to say.

First, you will note that the reconciliation is between *two persons* who have fallen out, and not between a failing person on the one hand and a perfect, imperturbable process on the other.

The second thing is a corollary from the first, and is that the reconciliation *affects and alters both parties* and not only one party. There was reconciliation on both sides.

Thirdly, it is a reconciliation which *rests upon atonement and redemption.*

Fourthly, it is a reconciliation of *the world as a cosmic whole.* The world as one whole; not a person here and another there, snatched as brands from the burning; not a group here and a group there; but the reconciliation of the whole world.

Fifthly, it is a reconciliation *final in Jesus Christ and His Cross,* done once for all; really effected in the spiritual world in such a way that in history the great victory is not still to be won; it has been won in reality, and has only to be followed up and secured in actuality. In the spiritual place, in Christ Jesus, in the divine nature, the victory has been won. That is what I mean by using the word "Final" at the close of the list.

I will expound these heads as I go along. Let me begin almost at the foundation and say this. Reconciliation has no moral meaning as between finite and infinite - none apart from the sense of guilt. The finished reconciliation, the setting up of the New Covenant by Christ, meant that human guilt was once for all robbed of its power to prevent the consummation of the Kingdom of God. It is the sense of guilt that we have to get back today for the soul's sake and the kingdom's; not simply the sense of sin. There are many who recognize the power of sin, the misfortune of it; what they do not recognize is the thing that makes it most sinful, which makes it what it is before God, namely, guilt; which introduces something noxious and not merely deranged, malignant and not merely hostile; the fact that it is transgression against not simply God, not simply against a loving God, but against a holy God. Everything begins and ends in our Christian theology with the holiness of God. That is the idea we have to get back into our current religious thinking. We have been living for the last two or three generations, our most progressive side has been living, upon the love of God, God's love to us. And it was very necessary that it should be appreciated. Justice had not been done to it. But we have now to take a step further, and we have to saturate our people in the years that are to come as thoroughly with the idea of God's *holiness* as they have been saturated with the idea of God's love. I have sometimes thought when preaching that I saw a perceptible change come over my audience when I turned from speaking about the love of God to speak about the holiness of God. There was a certain indescribable relaxing of interest, as though their faces should say, "What, have we not had enough of these incorrigible and obtrusive theologians who will not let us rest with the love of God but must go on talking about things that are so remote and professional as His holiness!" All that has to be changed. We have to stir the interest of our congregations as much with the holiness of God as the Church was stirred - first with the justice and then latterly with the love of God. It is the holiness of God which makes sin guilt. It is the holiness of God that necessitates the work of Christ, that calls for it, and that provides it. What is the great problem? The great problem in connection with atonement is not simply to show how it was necessary to the fatherly love, but how it was necessary to a holy love, how a holy love not only must have it but must make it. The problem is how Christ can be a revelation not of God's love simply, but of God's holy love. Without a holy God there would be not problem of atonement. It is the holiness of God's love that necessitates the atoning Cross.

I say, then, that the reconciliation has no meaning apart from guilt which must stir the anger of a holy God and produce separation from Him. That is, the reconciliation rests upon a justification, upon an atonement. Those were the great Pauline ideas which were rediscovered in the fifteenth and sixteenth centuries and became the backbone of the Reformation. They were practically rediscovered. Look at the movement in the history of the Church's thought in this respect. You have three great points: you might name them - the first from Augustine, the second from Luther; for the third, our modern time, we have as yet no such outstanding name. The first great movement towards the rediscovery of Paul was by Augustine. Do you know that Paul went under after the first century? He went under for historic reasons I cannot stay to explain. It is a remarkable thing how he was kept in the canon of Scripture. Paul went under, and for centuries remained under, and he had to be rediscovered. That was done by Augustine. Again he went under, and Luther rediscovered him. And he is being rediscovered again today. Augustine's rediscovery was this, justification by grace alone; Luther's side of the rediscovery was justification by faith alone - faith in the Cross, that is to say, faith in grace. What is our modern point of emphasis? Justification by holiness and for it alone. That is to say, as I have already pointed out, reconciliation is something that comes from the whole holy God, and it covers the whole of life, and it is not exhausted by the idea of atonement only or redemption only. It is the new-created race being brought to permanent, vital, life-deep communion with the holy God. Only holiness can be in communion with the holy God. We have to be saved - not indeed from morality, because we can only be saved by the moral; that is the grand sheet-anchor of our modern theories. However we be saved, we can only be saved in a way consistent with God's morality - that is to say, with holiness. The rescue is not from morality; but it is from mere moralism, from a religion three parts conduct. We are saved through the Spirit of a new life, an indiscerptible life in Jesus Christ. That is the grand new thing in Christianity (2 Corinthians 3:6)

Reconciliation, then, has no meaning apart from a sense of guilt, that guilt which is involved in our justification. I am going to try to expound that before I am done. I want to note here that it means not so much that God is reconciled, but that God is the Reconciler. It is the neglect of that truth which has produced so much skepticism in the matter of the atonement. So much of our orthodox religion has come to talk as though God were reconciled by a third party. We lose sight of this great central verse, "God was in Christ reconciling the world unto Himself." As we are both living persons, that means that there was reconciliation on God's side as well as ours; but wherever it was, it was effected by God Himself in Himself. In what sense was God reconciled within Himself? We come to that surely as we see that the first charge upon reconciling grace is to put away guilt, reconciling by not imputing trespasses. Return to our cardinal verse, 2 Corinthians 5:19. In reconciliation the ground for God's wrath or God's judgment was put away. Guilt rests on God's charging up sin; reconciliation rests upon God's non-imputation of sin; God's non-imputation of sin rests upon Christ being made sin for us. You have thus three stages in this magnificent verse. God's reconciliation rested upon this, that on His Eternal Son, who knew no sin in His experience, (although He knew more about sin than any man who has ever lived), sin's judgment fell. Him who knew no sin by experience, God made sin. That is to say, God by Christ's own consent identified Him with sin in treatment though not in feeling. God did not judge Him, but judged sin upon His head. He never once counted Him sinful; He was always well pleased with Him; it was part, indeed, of His own holy self-complacency. Christ was made sin for us, as He could never have been if He had been made a sinner. It was sin that had to be judged, more even than the sinner, in a world-salvation; and God made Christ sin in this sense, that God as it were took Him in the place of sin, rather than of the sinner, and judged the sin upon Him; and in putting Him there He really put Himself there in our place (Christ being what He was); so that the divine judgment of sin was real and effectual. That is, it fell where it was perfectly understood, owned, and praised, and had the sanctifying effect of judgment, the effect of giving holiness at last its own. God made Him to be sin in treatment though not in feeling, so that holiness might be perfected in judgment, and we might become the righteousness of God in Him; so that we might have in God's sight righteousness by our living union with Christ, righteousness which did not belong to us actually, naturally, and finally. Our righteousness is as little ours individually as the sin on Christ was His. The thief on the cross, for instance - I do not suppose he would have turned what we call a saint if he had survived; though saved, he would not have become sinless all at once. And the great saint, Paul, had sin working in him long after his conversion. Yet by union with Christ they were made God's righteousness, they were integrated into the New Goodness; God made them partakers of His eternal love to the ever-holy Christ. That is a most wonderful thing. Men like Paul, and far worse men than Paul, by the grace of God, and by a living faith, become partakers of that same eternal love which God from everlasting and to everlasting bestowed upon His only-begotten Son. It is beyond words.

It was not a case of wiping a slate. Sin is graven in. You cannot wipe off sin. It goes into the tissue of the spiritual being. And it alters things for both parties. Guilt affected both God and man. It was not a case of destroying an unfortunate prejudice we had against God. It was not a case of putting right a misunderstanding we had of God. "You are afraid of God," you hear easy people say; "it is a great mistake to be afraid of God. There is nothing to be afraid of. God is love." But there is everything in the love of God to be afraid of. Love is not holy without judgment. It is the love of holy God that is the consuming fire. It was not simply a case of changing our method, or thought, our prejudices, or the moral direction of our soul. It was not a case of giving us courage when we were cast down, showing us how groundless our depression was. It was not that. If that were all it would be a comparatively light matter.

If that were all, Paul could only have spoken about the reconciliation of single souls, not about the reconciliation of the whole world as a unity. He could not have spoken about a finished reconciliation to which every age of the future was to look back as its glorious and fontal past. In the words of that verse which I am constantly pressing, "God was in Christ reconciling the world unto Himself." Observe, first, "the world" is the unity which corresponds to the reconciled unity of "Himself"; and second, that He was not trying, not taking steps to provide means of reconciliation, not opening doors of reconciliation if we would only walk in at them, not laboring toward reconciliation, not (according to the unhappy phrase) waiting to be gracious, but "God was in Christ reconciling," actually reconciling, finishing the work. It was not a tentative, preliminary affair (Romans 11:15). Reconciliation was finished in Christ's death. Paul did not preach a gradual reconciliation. He preached what the old divines used to call the finished work. He did not preach a gradual reconciliation which was to become the reconciliation to the world only piecemeal, as men were induced to accept it, or were affected by the gospel. He preached something done once for all - reconciliation which is the base of every soul's reconcilement, not an invitation only. What the Church has to do is to appropriate the thing that has been finally and universally done. We have to enter upon the reconciled position, on the new creation. Individual men have to enter upon that reconciled position, that new covenant, that new relation, which already, in virtue of Christ's Cross, belonged to the race as a whole. I will even use for convenience' sake the word totality. (People turn up their noses at a word like that they say it smells of philosophy. Well, philosophy has not a bad smell! You cannot have a proper theology unless you have a philosophy. You cannot accurately express the things that theology handles most deeply. The misfortune of our ministry is that it comes to theology without the proper preliminary culture - with a pious or literary culture only.) I am going to use this word totality, and say that the first bearing of Christ's work was upon the race as a totality. The first thing reconciliation does is to change man's corporate relation to God. Then when it is taken home individually it changes our present attitude. Christ, as it were, put us into the eternal Church; the Holy Spirit teaches us how to behave properly in the Church.

I go on to show that reconciliation has its effect not upon man only, but upon God also. That is a difficulty to many people. And, indeed, we require to be somewhat discriminating here. If you say bluntly that Christ reconciled God, it is more false than true. I do not say it is untrue. It is the people who want plain black and white, false or true, that do so much mischief in these matters. It is the thin, commonsense rationalists, orthodox or heterodox. It is the people who put a pistol to your head and say, "I am a plain man and I want a plain yes or no," that cause so much difficulty. Christ always refused to answer with a pistol to His head. It was the whole manner of His ministry to refuse to give a plain answer when asked a blunt question. We see that in Peter's discovery and confession, "Thou art the Christ," and in Christ's joyful answer, "Blessed Simon." Peter in his confession had crowned what Christ had labored to live in upon them, but what He had never said plainly in so many words - "I am the Christ." He lived it into them and made them discover it. Repeatedly He was asked, "Give us signs," "Give us yes or no," and He always refused. That would be sight, not faith. A plain yes or no is sight. But faith is insight into Christ. In this region a plain yes or no is somewhat out of place. So, therefore, while it is not false to say that Christ reconciled God, it is more false than true as it is mostly put. You do not get it in the Bible. It would be a useful exercise to go through the Bible and see what proofs you can get of Christ reconciling God. If we talk about Christ reconciling God in the way some do, we suggest that there was some third party coming between us and God, reconciling God on the one hand and us on the other, like a daysman. That is one great mischief that is done by the popular theories of atonement. God can never be regarded as the object of some third party's intervention in reconciling. If it were so, what would happen? There would be no grace. It would be a bought thing, a procured thing, the work of a pardon-broker; and the one essential thing about grace is that it is unbought and unpurchasable. It is the freest thing in heaven or earth. It would not be free if procured by some third party. The "daysman" metaphor has been much abused. It is a Scriptural figure, but we get it in the Old Testament, in Job, the idea being that of one who, in the case of a dispute, puts one hand on one head and the other on another and brings two persons together. That is a crude version of the Christian idea of reconciliation. The grace of God would not then be the prime and moving cause. It would not be spontaneous and creative, it would be negotiated grace; and that is a contradiction in terms. Mediation can never mean that. In paganism the gods were mollified. God, our God, could never be mollified. There is no mollification of God, no placation of God. Atonement was not the placating of God's anger. Even in the old economy we are told, "I have *given* you the blood to make atonement." Given! Did you ever see the force of it? "I have given you the blood to make atonement. This is an institution which I set up for you to comply with, set it up for purposes of My own, on principles of My own, but it is My gift." The Lord Himself provided the lamb for the burnt offering. Atonement in the Old

Testament was not the placating of God's anger, but the sacrament of God's grace. It was the expression of God's anger on the one hand and the expressing and putting in action of God's grace on the other hand. The effect of atonement was to cover sin from God's eyes, so that it should no longer make a visible breach between God and His people. The actual ordinance was established, they held, by God Himself. He covered the sin. Sacrifices were not desperate efforts and surrenders made by terrified people in the hope of propitiating an angry deity. The sacrifices were in themselves prime acts of obedience to God's means of grace and His expressed will. If you want to follow that out further, perhaps I may be forgiven if I were to allude to the last chapter in my book, "The Cruciality of the Cross" (1909), in which there is a fuller discussion of the particular point, and especially what is morally meant by the blood of Christ.

But some one immediately asks, Is there then no objective atonement? It is a question worth deep attention. A great many people say Christianity wrecks chiefly on the idea of objective atonement. How cheap the objection is in many cases, how easy and common it is! If you find somebody who is making it his mission in life to pull to pieces the venerable theology of the Catholic Church, and show how poor a thing it is in the light of the thirty years in which he has lived, you will hear it put likely enough in such terms as these: that objective atonement is sheer paganism. The Christian idea of atonement is identified offhand with the pagan idea of atonement, as a Hyde Park lecturer might. And when you have done that at the outset, it is the simplest thing to show how false and absurd and pagan such theology is. It is said further, that the whole Church has become paganized in this way, and has spoken as though God could be mollified by something offered to Him. The criticism is sometimes ignorant, sometimes ungenerous, sometimes culpable. If such language has ever been held, it has only been by sections of the Church, sections that have gone wrong in the direction of unqualified extremes. You have extravagances, remember, even in rational heresy. Has the Church on the whole ever really forgotten that it is in the mercy of God that all our hopes begin and end? And even if the Church had gone further wrong than it has done about this, we do not live upon the Church, but upon the gospel and upon the Bible. We live in and through the Church. We cannot do without it. We must get back a great deal more respect for it. But we do not live on the Church; we live on the word of the gospel which is in the Bible.

What is the real objective element in the Bible's gospel? What is the real objective element in atonement? We are tempted, I say, to declare that it was the offering of a sacrifice to God outside of Him and us, the offering of a sacrifice to God by somebody not God yet more than a single man. That is the natural, the pagan notion of objective atonement. But the real meaning of an objective atonement is that God Himself made the complete sacrifice. The real objectivity of the atonement is not that it was made to God, but by God. It was atonement made by God, not by man. When I use the word objective, I do not mean objective to you or to me. You are objective to me, and I to you. That is not the idea. Let us learn to thing on the scale of the whole race. What is objective to that? The deadly kind of subjectivity is the kind that is engrossed with individuals, or with humanity, and does not allow for God. It is the egotism of the race. And the real objectivity is that which is objective to the whole human race, over against it, and not merely facing you or me within it. The real objective element in the atonement, therefore, is that God made it and gave it finished to man, not that it was made to God by man. Any atonement made by man would be subjective, however much it might be made for man by his brother, or by a representative of entire Humanity.

But we have a certain farther difficulty to face here. If it was God that made the atonement - which it certainly was in Christianity - then was it not made to man? Can God reconcile Himself? And can the atonement mean anything more than the attuning of man to God - that is to say, of individual men in their subjective experience? God then says to each soul, "Be reconciled. See, I have put My anger away." Can such attuning of Himself by God have for its results anything more than individual conversion? Now, conversion means much, but it does not mean the whole of Christianity. Reconciliation means the life-communion of the race. But, if God made the atonement, it might seem that the result and effect of this atonement could only be reached gradually by the attuning of individual men to God. It would seem to destroy the totality of the race, or (to employ another word even more useful) the solidarity of the race. That would seem to be the effect; and it is such a serious effect, for this reason: that it affects the universality of Christ's work. Whatever affects the universality of Christ's work cuts the ground from under aggressive Christianity, from under missions, whether at home or abroad. They cannot thrive except upon a faith which means the universality of Christ's work, which means again the solidarity, the organic unity, of the whole human race. And the conversion of a race is a work that exceeds conversion and is redemption. About that the Old Testament and the New Testament are at one.

But, you say, you do not have the solidarity of the human race in the Old Testament. Well, you do, and you do not. What you have fact to face with God in the Old Testament is a collective nation, Israel. We shall never read the Old Testament with true understanding until we realize that. That is one of the great things modern scholarship has brought home to us - that the *vis-a-vis* of God in the Old Testament is Israel and not the individual Jew. Gradually, as the Old Testament develops in spiritual intimacy, you have this changing and becoming intensely individual, as in the later Psalms. In Jeremiah it became so especially. The greatest prefiguration of Christ's individual solitude in the Old Testament is Jeremiah. But both of them were representative or collective individuals. They condensed the people. The object that faced God in the God in the Old Testament in the main was not primarily the individual soul, it was the soul of the nation of Israel, even though it was sometimes reduced to a remnant. What took place when Israel made the great refusal of Christ? There was set up another collective unity, the Church, the new Israel, the spiritual Israel, the landless, homeless Israel, whose home was in Him, the universal Israel, the new Humanity of the new covenant. The Church became the prophecy and prefiguration of the unity of Humanity. It is through the Church alone that the unity of Humanity can be consummated, because it is possible only through the gospel. And the preacher of this gospel in the world is the collective Church.

We must, therefore, avoid every idea of atonement which seems to reduce it to God's dealing with a mass of individuals instead of with the race as a whole - instead of a racial, a social, a collective salvation, in which alone each individual has his place and part. Our Protestant theology has been too individualist, too little collectivist. And that has had serious social consequences as well as theological. The basis of a social salvation is the final redemption in one act of the total race. And that act was the Cross of Christ.

IV. Reconciliation, Atonement, and Judgment

The point at which I broke off yesterday was this. I was pointing out that objective atonement is absolutely necessary. Of course, it is quite necessary also that we should know what is meant by an objective atonement. The real objective element in atonement is not that something was offered to God, but that God made the offering. And in this connection I hinted that my remarks today and tomorrow would have to follow the idea also, that God's atonement initially was made on behalf of the race, and on behalf of individuals in so far as they were members of the race. The first charge upon Christ and His Cross was the reconciliation of the race, and of its individuals by implication.

We start today, then, from the position that God made the atonement. This (we saw) suggests a number of questions, not to say difficulties. If God made the atonement, but reconciliation meant no more than simply the moving and attuning of individual men in their subjective experience, it might seem as though it destroyed the solidarity of mankind and made it granular. And the peril there is that whatever destroys that, destroys the universality of Christ's work. But that atomism is not the Gospel. To reduce the reconciliation merely to the aggregate of individual conversions would be a total misrepresentation of New Testament reconciliation, which is both solidary and final.

Then there is another difficulty. If we say that the one object of the atonement was not the reconciliation of God, but the reconciliation of man to God, then it looks as though the work of Christ became only the grand heliograph from divine heights, the chief word in what I might call a language of signs; as though it were only the leading expression of God's will towards men, instead of something actually done, and not merely said or shown, by God, something really done from the depth of God Who is the action of the world, something eternally changing the whole situation, and destiny, and responsibility of our race. If God in Christ simply said the most powerful word about His goodwill, His placability, and His permanence of Christ - the depth of His work, and the height of His place. Thus God would be *saying* more than He *did*; and we have a natural and proper difficulty in thoroughly trusting people who say more than they do. If Christ were simply an expression of God's love, then His Cross would simply be what is called an object-lesson of God's love; or it would simply be a witness to the serious way in which God takes man's sin; or it might even be nor more than the expression of the strong conviction of Jesus about it. We are exposed to the danger there always is when we make revelation a word rather than a deed, something said instead of something done, when we make it manifestation only and redemption. The work of Christ would be only something educational, or at most impressive. And what happens then? If the work of Christ is only impressively educational, if the need and value of it ceases when we have recognized its meaning, when we have taken God's word for it in Christ that He does really love us, what happens then? Why, as soon as the lesson had been learnt, the work of Christ might be left behind. There are a great many people today who are Christian in a way, but have very loose ideas as to what is involved centrally in their Christianity. Many of them are in this position I describe - they think they can ignore Christ and the work of Christ since they have assimilated the lesson these taught. If the Cross is a kind of practical parable which God set forth of His love and His willingness to save, then when the parable has done its work it can be forgotten. When the lesson has been taught, the example can be put away into the school store-room until we want it again. It is exhausted for the time being, until somebody else comes who needs the same lesson. In that case the work of Christ simply sinks to the level of other valuable events in the history of religion. It is not fontal but episodic. It represents the transition from Judaism to a religion of Humanity. It represents a great movement in the history of religion, when religion ceased to be national and particularist, and became universal, when it ceased to be ritual and became spiritual. The death of Christ would thus be a great monument in the past, which fades out of sight as we surmount it and leave it behind; and it does not retain a permanent meaning and function at the center of our faith.

I said that the work of Christ meant not only an action on man, it meant an action on God. Yet I pointed out that it was more false than true to say that Christ and His death reconciled God to man. I said that we must in some way construe the matter as God reconciling Himself. It was out of the question to think of any reconciliation effected upon God by a third party standing between God and man. God could not be reconciled by man nor by one neither God nor man. The only alternative, therefore, is that God should reconcile Himself. But then is there not something in that which seems a little forced and unnatural? Did God have to compel Himself to change His feeling about us? Did He force Himself to be gracious? There is something wrong here surely, something that needs adjustment, explanation, restatement in some way.

Are we obliged to suppose that if God did reconcile Himself it was in the sense of changing His own heart and affection towards us? I have pointed out that the heart of God towards us, His gracious disposition towards us, was from His own holy eternity; that grace is of the unchangeable. God in that respect had not to be changed. Was He changed at all then? If His heart was not changed, what remained in Him to be changed, what was changed in connection with the work of Christ?

There was a change. And I am going to ask you to recognize here another of those valuable distinction of which the man without the evangelical experience and its theological discipline is so impatient. As I work my way through the difficulties and questions that present themselves, over and over again I perceive that many of the difficulties that seem so serious to some turn entirely upon some valuable distinction that has been ignored, often for lack of deep religion or due professional education. Of course the man in the street says, as soon as he is asked to distinguish, that that is getting into the region of subtleties. Never mind the man in the street. The distinguished person for him is the person with the least distinction from himself, the person who gives him most satisfaction with least trouble, the person who works in black and white with no shades. Besides, the man in the street is not devoted to his Bible, nor to getting into the interior of the Bible, as you preachers are. We must take our way, God's way, and follow the subtle and searching Holy Spirit as He leads and speaks in and through the questions that arise to our earnest thought concerning Christ's death. And the man in the street must be left to the grace which has taken us in from the street.

The distinction I ask you to observe is between a change of feeling and a change of treatment, between affection and discipline, between friendly feeling and friendly relations. God's feeling toward us never needed to be changed. But God's treatment of us, God's practical relation to us - that had to change. I have pointed out that the relation between God and man in reconciliation is a personal one, and that, where you have real personal relation and personal communion, if there is change on one side there must be change on the other. The question is as to the nature of the change. We have barred out the possibility of its being a change of affection, of hatred into grace. God never ceased to love us even when He was most angry and severe with us. It will not do to abolish the reality of God's anger towards us. True love is quite capable of being angry, and must be angry and even sharp with its beloved children. Let us fix our attention more closely upon this distinction of mood and manner.

Take the parable of the prodigal for illustration. There are those who say you have the whole of the gospel really in the parable of the prodigal son, that that was the culmination of Christ's grand revelation of God. Well, if that were so the wonder to me is, first, that the apostles never seem to have used it; and, second, that having delivered this parable Christ did not at once consider His mission discharged and return to heaven. Or, on the other hand, why did He not continue to live to a ripe and useful age, reiterating in various forms and in different settings this waiting (but inert) love and grace of God? We are moved sometimes to think He might have done well had He not provoked death so early, had He remained, like John, to seventy or ninety years of age continually publishing, applying, and spreading the message which He gave His disciples. But you have not the whole gospel in the parable of the prodigal son. What is the function of a parable? It is one of the great discoveries and lessons taught us by modern scholarship, that parables are not allegories, because they exist for the sake of one central idea. While we may allow ourselves, under the suggestion of the Holy Spirit to receive hints of edifying truth from this or the other phase or detail of the parable, we have chiefly to ask, What was it in the mind of Christ for the sake of which He uttered this parable? Each parable puts in an ample ambit one central idea. Now the one ruling idea in the parable of the prodigal son is the idea of the centrality, the completeness, the unreservedness, the freeness, fullness, whole-heartedness of God's grace - the absolute fullness of it, rather that the method of its action. But however a parable might preach that fullness, it took the Cross and all its train to give it effect, to put it into action, life, and history, to charge it with the Spirit. Those who tell us that the whole gospel is embodied in the parable say, You observe nothing is suggested in the parable about the Cross and the Atonement; therefore the Cross and the Atonement are subsequent and gratuitous additions, confusing the gospel of grace. But that turns Christ into a mere preacher, instead of the center of the world's history. Bear in mind also that this parable was spoken by the Christ who had the Cross in the very structure of His personality as its vocation, and at the root, therefore, of all His words. That Cross was deep embedded in the very structure of Christ's Person, because nowadays you cannot separate His Person from His vocation, from the work He came to do, and the words He came to speak. The Cross was not simply a fate awaiting Christ in the future; it pervaded subliminally His holy Person. He was born for the Cross. It was His genius, His destiny. If was quite inevitable that, in a world like this, One holy as Jesus was holy should come to the Cross. The parable was spoken by One in whom the Cross and all it stands for were latent in His idea of God; and it became patent, came to the surface, became actual, and practical, and powerful in the stress of man's crisis and the fullness of God's time. That is an important phrase. Christ Himself came in a fullness of time. The Cross which consummated and crowned Christ came in its fullness of time. The time was not full during Christ's life for preaching an atonement that life could never make. Hence as to the *method* of God's free and flowing grace the parable has nothing to say. It does not even say that the father was seeking the prodigal. The seeking grace of God we find there as little as the redeeming grace. And so also you have not the mode of grace's action *on a world*. But, speaking of what you do have in the parable, the father knows no change of feeling towards the prodigal; yet could he go on making no difference? Could he go on treating the prodigal as though he never had become a prodigal? He did not certainly when he returned; and as little could he before. His heart followed the prodigal, but his relations, his confidence, his intercourse were with his brother. So long as the son is prodigal he cannot be treated as though he were otherwise. Even repentance needs some guarantee of permanence. The father's heart is the same, but his treatment must be different. Cases have been known where the father had to expel the black sheep from the family for the sake of the others. Loving the poor creature all the same, he yet found it quite impossible, in the interests of the whole family, to treat him as though he were like the rest. So God needed no placation, but He could not exercise His kindness to the prodigal world, He certainly could not restore communion with its individuals, without doing some act which permanently altered the relation. And this is what set up that world's reconciliation with Him. It was set up by an act of crisis, of judgment.

Remember always we are dealing with the world in the first instance and not with individuals. I constantly come back upon that, for the orthodox and their critics forget it alike. I suppose the prodigal was a slave, I suppose he had sold himself to that vile work of swine-feeding. When he returned I suppose he ran away from his master. But the prodigal world, of course, could not run away from its master, it could not run away from the power that it was enslaved to. "Myself am hell." Supposing now the prodigal had not been able to run away. Supposing he had been guarded as a convict is guarded, then he could only come back by being bought of. As soon as you go beyond the one theme of the parable, the absolute heartiness of grace, and begin to think of grace's methods with a world, this point must be faced by all who are more than pooh-pooh sentimentalists in their religion. We have to deal with a world in a bondage it could not break. If the prodigal could not have arisen to go to his father; if the elder brother had sold up the whole farm, reduced himself to poverty, taken the sum in his hand, followed the prodigal into the far country, and there spent the whole amount in buying his brother's manumission from his master before a judge; and if it was all done by mutual purpose and consent of himself and his father; would not that act be a great and effective thing, not so much in producing repentance but in a harder matter - in destroying a lien and making absolute certainty of the father's forgiveness? He is sure because the father not only says but pays. His mere repentance could not make him sure, could not place him at home again, could not put him where he set out. His mere repentance could turn his heart to his father, but it could not break the bar and fill him with certainty of his father's love and forgiveness. And that is what the sinner wants, and what the great and classic penitents find it so hard to believe. Now, the parable tells us of the freeness of God's grace, and its fullness, but the Cross enacts it and inserts it in really history. It shows to what length that grace could go in dealing with a difficulty otherwise insuperable when we turn from a single prodigal to a world. The act which I have described by a New Testament extension of the parable - the act of Christ's Cross - is not simply to produce individual repentance, but it has its great effect upon the relation of the whole world to God. And the judgment, the payment, was on that scale. I will show you later that it was not pain that was paid but holy obedience.

What the elder brother does in the supposition I have made is twofold. First, he secures the liberation, he deals with the equitable conditions of the release. Secondly, he also acts upon the prodigal's heart and confidence. In the first case he meets certain judicial conditions, certain social conditions, ethical conditions, bound up with the existing order, the law of society in which the prodigal was living. But it is said sometimes that there the analogy fails, because the elder son, acting for the father, in my extension of the story, has to deal with a law which is outside his control and outside the father's control; he has to deal with the law of society, with the law of the land where the prodigal was. Whereas, if you come to think about God, there can be no social and moral conditions which are outside His control. There, it is said, your illustration breaks down. God could ignore any such impediments at His loving will. Now, that is just the crucial mistake that you make, that even Kant does not allow us to make. God could do nothing of the kind. So far the omnipotence of God is a limited omnipotence. He could not trifle with His own holiness. He could will nothing against His holy nature, and He could not abolish the judgment bound up with it. Nothing in the compass of the divine nature could enable Him to abolish a moral law, the law of holiness. That would be tampering with His own soul. It had to be dealt with. Is the law of God more loose than the law of society? Can it be taken liberties with, played with, and put aside at the impulse even of love? How little we should come to think of God's love if that were possible! How essential the holiness of that love is to our respect for it and our faith in its unchangeableness! It God's love were not essentially holy love, in course of time mankind would cease to respect it, and consequently to trust it. We need not a fond love, but a love we can trust, and for ever. What love wants is not simply love in response, but respect and confidence. In the bringing up of children today one often wishes they had more training in respect, even if less in affection. God's holy law is His own holy nature. His love is under the condition of eternal respect. It is quite unchangeable. It is just as much outside His operation, so far as abrogation goes, as was the law of the far country to the father of the prodigal.

What was there in the work of Christ which went beyond a mere impressive declaration of a God who could not help being gracious, but fell on the prodigal's neck without more ado? It was solidary judgment. I am urging that the difficulty we have in answering that questions is due to our modern individualism. Individualism has done its work for Christianity for the time being, and we are now suffering from its after-effects. We do not realize that we are each one of us saved in a racial salvation. We are each one of us saved in the salvation of the race, in a collectivist redemption. What Christ saved was the whole human race. What He bought, if we may provisionally use the metaphor, was the Church, and not any aggregate of isolated souls. So great is a soul, and so great is its sin, that each man is only saved by an act which at the same time saves the whole world. If you reduce or postpone Christ's effect upon the totality of the world, you are in the long run preparing the way for a poor estimate of the human soul. The more you abolish the significance of Christ's redeeming death once for all, the more you are doing to lower Humanity morally, and make it a less precious thing than the cosmic world around us. My plea is that with no atonement, no solidary judgment of sin, you reduce reconciliation not only to sentiment but to a piecemeal series of individual repentances and conversions, leaving it a problem whether the race as a whole will be saved at last. For the universality of Christianity (so dear to Broad Church) you must have that foregone finality which the New Testament offers in the atonement.

I pointed out to you that in the Old Testament, for the most part, what faced God was not this prophet or that saint, this king or that particular juncture, but Israel. I said that in the subsequent phases of Jewish religion, indeed, that idea has its detail filled in; and in the later psalms, in many of those psalms which we know could only have been written after the captivity, you have pious individualism sometimes expressing itself very strongly. But there the two warring notes were - new individualism and old collectivism; and between these there never came complete reconcilement until Christ came and Christ's work. What have we in that great text, John 3:16? "God so loved *the world*" - the world was the prime object of God's love - "God so loved the world, that He gave His only begotten Son, that *whosoever* believeth on Him should not perish but have eternal life." Love in the first instance directed upon the world, but directed upon the world in such a way that it should be taken home in every individual experience. Mark the two words, "the world" and "whosoever". Dwell upon the contrast. God loved not this or that individual, or group of individuals, only. "God so loved the world" that He did something to it in such a way that every individual "whosoever" should receive the benefit, and receive it in the only way which made a world of saved individuals possible. You can never compound a saved world out of any number of saved individuals. But God did so save the world as to carry individual salvation in the same act. The Son of God was not an individual merely; He was the representative of the whole race, and its *vis-a-vis,* on its own scale. So that, in Ephesians, the Church, in rising to Christ, had to acquire the fullness of a complete and colossal man. No individual prophet of salvation could save the world. He could not be capable of a pity great enough, or a love. The world could only be saved by somebody as large as the world, and indeed larger. If he could not save the world he could make no *eternal* salvation of any individual. It is universal, eternal salvation every way - universal not by the addition of all units, but in a solidary sense. What we are tempted to think of in our common version of Christianity is a mass of people, great or small, a mass of individuals, each one of whom makes his own terms with God and gets discharge of his sin. It is salvation by private bargain. In conversion every individual makes his own peace with God through Jesus Christ, so that the work of God becomes a mere change of attitude, feeling, or temper of the side of man after man. That is not the New Testament idea.

Again, in speaking of the change in God, Christ has been represented as enabling God to forgive by enabling Him to adjust His two attributes of justice and mercy within Himself. Some theologians of the Reformation - Melancthon for one - spoke of Christ in that fashion. But we have entirely outgrown that way of thinking and talking about it. It has produced much difficulty and scepticism. What does it proceed upon? It proceeds upon a certain definition of an attribute, as though an attribute were something loose within God which He could manipulate - as though the attributes of God were not God Himself, unchangeable God, in certain relations. The attributes of God are not things within Himself which He could handle and adjust. An attribute of God is God Himself behaving, with all His unity, in a particular way in a particular situation. God is a thinking God, let us say. He has the attribute of thought. Does that mean that the attribute of thought could be taken away, that God could divest Himself of it? No. The thought of God is simply God thinking. So also the love of God is not an attribute of God; it is God loving. The holiness of God is not an attribute of God; it is the whole God Himself as holy. There is nothing in the Bible about the strife of attributes. Rather remember 1 John 1:9, "He is faithful and just to forgive us our sins." It is in the exercise of His faithfulness to Himself and His observance of justice that He should forgive. It lies in the very holiness that condemns. There is a similar text in the Psalms, "Thou art merciful; Thou givest to every man according to his work." He is the faithful and just to forgive. There needed no adjustment of His justice with His forgiveness. So also in Isaiah, "A just God and a Savior." There can be therefore be no strife of attributes.

What, then, does it mean when we hear about the anger of God being turned away? To begin with, the anger of God means a great deal more than His passion, His temper, His mode of feeling, more than anger as an affection. The anger of God in the Bible means much rather the judgment of God in the reaction of His moral and spiritual order. The judgment of God is perfectly compatible with His continued love, just as a father's punishment is perfectly compatible with his love for his children. The father has to discipline his children. He institutes certain laws, the children disobey; they must be punished, or, using the more dignified term, judged. The anger of God: we shall get the most meaning out of it when we think of it as the judgment of God, the exalted, inflexible judgment of God.

Taking a step further, it is judgment on the world. It seems at first sight as though it were meaningless to speak as if God could be wroth with the world and yet gracious and loving to individuals. But I may be very angry with a political party, yet I cherish respect and love for individuals belonging to that party. We must be on our guard against narrow, individual views, against treating individuals according to their public and collective condemnation. We are created, redeemed, judged as members of a race or of a Church. Salvation is personal, but it is not individual. (There is another distinction for you, if you have come in off the street.) It is personal in its appropriation but collective in its nature. What did the Reformation stand for? Not for religious individualism. But I hear some one asking in the back of his mind, Was not the Reformation the charter of private judgment and individual independence? It was nothing of the kind. It was the charter of personal direct faith and its freedom. What the Reformation did was to turn religion from being a thing mainly institutional into a thing mainly personal. The reformers were as strong as their opponents about the necessity of the Church for the soul - though as its home, not its master. They were not individualists. Individualism is fatal to faith. It was the backbone of the rationalism and atheism of the French Revolution. The Reformation stands for personal religion and social religion and not for religious individualism.

There is no such thing as an absolute individual. What is the change that takes place when we are converted? Our change is really from one membership to another, from membership of the world to membership of the Church. When we become a member of the Church we are not really changed from individualism, but from membership of the world. It is membership either way. The greatest egoist and self-seeker is a member of the world. He could not indulge his egotism if it were not for the society in the midst of which he lives and into which he is articulated. He is a member of the world who exploits his membership instead of serving with it. When we are converted we are not converted from a sheer and absolute individual. There never was such a person. Certainly Robinson Crusoe was not. We are converted from membership of the world to membership of Christ. Before our conversion and after we *belong*. We are not absolute, solitary individuals. We are in a society, an organism. We are made by the past. And our selfish, godless actions and influence go out, radiate, affect the organism as they could not do were we absolute units. They spread far beyond our memory or control. In the same way we are acted upon by the other people. We are members one of another both for evil and for good. When you are told that evil is only selfishness it is worth while bearing this in mind. Even as selfish men, as egoists, we belong - only to a pagan order instead of to Christ. The selfish man is a member of a kingdom of evil. There is no such thing as an absolute individual. Hence, to save us, to reconcile us, involves the whole race we belong to. Before God that race is an organic unity. It is not a mere mass of atoms joined together by various arbitrary relations, sympathies, and affinities. Hence, as the race before God is one, a personal God is able to do for the race some one thing which at the same time is good for every person in it.

But now, if the race is a unity, where does its unity lie? Does it lie in our elementary affections for each other, in the palpable relationships of natural life with our parents, brothers, lovers, and friends? Or is the unity of the race simply its capacity for being organized by skillful engineers? Is the unity of the race like the unity of machines? No. The unity of the race is a moral unity. Therefore it is a unity of conscience. If you want to find the trunk out of which all the loves and practices of humanity proceed, you must go to conscience at the center. That is where the unity of Humanity lies. It is in the conscience, where man is member of a vast moral world. It is the one changeless order of the moral world, emerging in conscience, that makes man universal. What have you to preach if you have no gospel that goes to the foundations of human conscience? What ground have you for a social religion? The most universal God is one that goes there, not to the heart in the sense of affections, but to the conscience. The great motive for missions of every high kind is not sentiment, but salvation. It is dangerous to take your theology from poets and literary people. You quote, "One touch of nature makes the whole world kin." Well, if you are going to build a religion on that, it will have a very short life. In the long run nature means anarchy when taken by and for itself. But it was never meant to be taken by itself. It was meant to go in an eternal context with super-nature. It is not the touch of nature that makes us kin enough for religion, for eternity, but the touch, and more than a touch, of the supernatural - not nature, but grace. What makes the world God's world is the action and unity of God's moral order of which our conscience speaks.

Now, if that order be broken, how can it be healed? If I slit the canvas of this tent it can be patched. I make a fissure, but it is not irremediable. I simply get some one to stitch it up. At the worst I can have a new width put in. But if the moral order, and its universal solidarity, its holiness, is broken, how can that be healed? That cannot be patched up. It is not merely a rent in a tissue, a gap in a process, which the same process goes on to heal into a scar. The moral law differs from all natural law in having in it a demand, a claim, an "ought" of a universal kind. It is all of one piece. We use the word "law" in a loose kind of way. We apply the same word to gravitation and to the moral law of retribution. It is that ambiguity of terms which leads us astray. The moral law differs from every other law in having a demand, and a universal demand, a claim upon us for ever. And that has to be made good as well as the rents and bruises in us from our own collision with it. It is not a gap that has to be made good and sound. It is a claim, because we are here in a moral and not a natural world. It is one thing to make good a gap and another thing to make good a claim. The claim must be met. It will not do simply to draw the edges together by mere amendment, to have God here and man there, and gradually bring them together till they unite. It is two moral persons with moral passions we have to do with. It is moral relationship that is in question, communion, trustful mutuality, is the object of the divine requirement. It is a case of moral, holy reconcilement. It is the expression of God's holy personality whenever God makes His claim. It is Himself in holy, changeless personality that says, "Thou shalt." Then the claim can only be honored by personality of acknowledgment. But what does that mean? Some confession, some compunction - "I have sinned?" That is a poor acknowledgment of God's holiness. It was neither in word nor in feeling that we wounded that, but in life and deed. It must be acknowledged in like fashion - practically. The holiness of God is the sum of all His action and relation to the world; and the acknowledgment of it must be made in like action. Do we acknowledge the holiness of God's infinite law simply when its penalty wrings from poor us a confession of sin? We acknowledge natural law in spite of ourselves when we suffer its penalty amid our rebellion. But the acknowledgment of moral, of holy law is something different. It must be actively acknowledged - acknowledged not in spite of ourselves but by ourselves, with our whole heart; and it cannot be acknowledged simply by individual, or, indeed, any suffering. For divine judgment it must be acknowledged in kind and scale, and met by a like holiness. Mere suffering is no acknowledgment really; it is a pure sequel; it is not a confession of the moral law and its righteousness, only of its power. Mere suffering is no confession of the holiness of God. God, truly, might and does assert His power upon our defiance by making us suffer. But do you think any holiness, any loving holiness, could be satisfied with making the offender suffer? There is only one thing that can satisfy the holiness of God, and that is holiness - adequate holiness. To judge is to secure that at cost of *any* pain both to the judge and the culprit. But the pain is not the end. Nothing, no penalty, no passionate remorse, no verbal acknowledgment, no ritual, can satisfy the claim of holy law - nothing but holiness, actual holiness, and holiness upon the same scale as the one holy law which was broken. The confession must be adequate. Fix that word in your mind. All your repentance, and all the world's repentance, would not be adequate to satisfying, establishing the broken law of holy God. Confession must be adequate - as Christ's was. We do not now speak of Christ's sufferings as being the *equivalent* of what we deserved, but we speak of His confession of God's holiness, his acceptance of God's judgment, being *adequate* in a way that sin forbade any acknowledgment from us to be. For the only adequate confession of a holy God is perfectly holy man. Wounded holiness can only be met by a personal holiness upon the scale of the race, upon the universal scale of the sinful race, and upon the eternal scale of the holy God who was wounded. It is not enough that the eternal validity of the holy law should be declared as some prophet might arise and declare it, with power to make the world admire, as the great and sublime Kant did. It must take effect. Prophets have arisen who have produced tremendous effect by insisting upon the moral ultimacy in life and things. The greatest prophets of the last century, like George Eliot, Carlyle, Ruskin, and Maurice among ourselves had that as a chief note. But it is not enough that the eternal validity and inflexibility of eternal law should be powerfully, searchingly declared. It must take effect. Its breach must be closed up not merely by recognition, but by judgment. It is not enough that the whole human race should come confessing, "We have offended against Thy holy law." That would recognize the holy law and confess its place, but it would not give it its own, it would not bring to pass that which is essential to holiness, namely, judgment. It would not actually establish holiness in a kingdom, in command of history. You cannot separate the idea of holiness and its kingdom from the idea of judgment. In the Old Testament the final coming of the Great Salvation was always connected with a great judgment, which was therefore not a terror, as we view it, but the grandest hope. If the essence of God is that He should be holy, it is equally essential that He should judge. If He sets up actual holiness it must be by actual adjustment of everything to it. It is not enough that we should say, "Thou art our Judge, we submit and are willing to take the penalty. The wages of sin is death." All that is best and greatest in human life turns upon something more than that. There is a phrase which I never tire of quoting, and it is this: "The dignity of man is better assured if he were broken upon the maintenance of that holiness of God than if it were put aside just to give him an existence." The dignity, the very dignity of man himself is better assured if he were broken upon the maintenance of that holiness of God than if it were put aside arbitrarily, just to let him off with his life. This holy order is as essential to man's greatness as it is to God's; and that is why the holy satisfaction Christ made to God's holiness is in the same act the glorifier of the new humanity. Any religion which leaves out of supreme count the judging holiness of God is making a great contribution to the degradation of man. We need a religion which decides the eternal destiny of man; and unless holiness were practically and adequately established - not merely recognized and eulogized, but established - there could be no real, deep, permanent change in the world or the sinner. The change in the treatment of us by eternal grace must rest on judgment taking effect. Man is not forgiven simply be forgetting and mending, by agreeing that no more is to be said about it. To make little of sin is to belittle the holiness of God; and from a reduced holiness no salvation could come, nor could human dignity remain.

Here, perhaps, you want to ask me what I mean exactly by saying that the judgment-death of Christ set up a real and actual kingdom of holiness. It is a point which it is easier for faith to realize than for theology to explain. But the answer would lie along this line: What Christ presented to God for His complete joy and satisfaction was a perfect racial obedience. It was not the perfect obedience of a saintly unit of the race. It was a racial holiness. God's holiness found itself again in the humbled holiness of Christ's "public person." He presented before God a race He created for holiness. Remember that the very nature of our faith in Christ is union with Him. The kingdom is set up by Christians being united with the work, the victory, the obedience, the holiness of the King. Christ, in His victorious death and risen life, has power to unite the race to Himself, and to work His complete holiness into its actual experience and history. He has power, by uniting us with Him in His Spirit, to reduce Time to acknowledge in act and fact His conclusive victory of Eternity. When you think of what He did for the race and its history, you must on no account do what the Church and its theology has too often done - you must no omit our living union with Him. It is not enough to believe that He gained a victory at a historic point. Christ is the condensation of history. You must go on to think of His summary reconciliation as being worked out to cover the whole of history and enter each soul by the Spirit. You must think of the Cross as setting up a new covenant and a new Humanity, in which Christ dwells as the new righteousness of God. "Christ for us" is only intelligible as "Christ in us" and we in Him. By uniting us to Himself and His resurrection in His Spirit He becomes the eternal guarantee of the historical consummation of all things some great day. I return to this later.

Sometimes, when I have been talking about this claim of God's holiness, a critic has said: "You are treating the holiness of God as though it were a power outside God, tying His hands." Nothing of the kind. What is meant by the holiness of God is the holy God. We talk nonsense in a like way about the decrees of God. We say they stand for the wretched survival of an outworn Calvinism, as though they were things that God could handle. Do you think that mighty men such as the great Reformers were would have been led into saying the things they did about God if they thought the decrees were simply things God could handle, or things like a doom on God? The decrees of God were to them God decreeing. The holiness of God was God as holy. When that holiness is wounded or defied, could God be content to take us back with a mere censure or other penance and the declaration that He was holy? We could not respect a God like that. Servants despise indulgent masters. Sinners would despise a God who would take us back when we wept, and speak thus: "Let us say no more about it. You did very wrong, and you have suffered for it, and I; but let us forget it now you have come back," We should not respect that. We should go on, as servants do in the case I have named, to take more liberties still. He would be a God who only talked His holiness and did not put it into force. Now, if our repentance were our atonement, and the Cross were simply an object-lesson to us of God's patient and tender mercy to penitence, He would be talking, I said, and not acting. He would mention the gravity of our sin very impressively, but that would not be establishing goodness actually in the history and experience of man. The sinner's reconciliation to a God of holy love could not take place if guilt were not destroyed, if judgment did not take place on due scale, if the wrath of God did not somehow take real effect. You say, perhaps, it did take effect in the unseen world of spirits. But the moral world is not a world of ghostly spirits. It is the unseen side of the world of history and of experience, it is its inner reality and center. The vindication, the judgment, must take place within human history and experience. It must take place in the terms of human history, by human action, in a place, at some point, on a due scale and with adequate depth. That was what took place in the Cross of Christ. The idea of judgment is not complete without the idea of a crisis, a day of judgment. Now the Cross of Christ was the world's great day of judgment, the crisis of all crises for history. The holy love of God yearning over souls could not deal with individual sinners, there was a cloud between God and the race, till the holiness was owned and perfectly praised by its racial confession, until holiness was confessed much more than sin, until on man's side there was not only confession of sin but confession of holiness from sin's side amid the experience of a judgment on the scale of the race, until the confessing race was thus put in right relation to God's holiness. Then judgment had done its perfect work. The race's sin was covered and atoned by it, *i.e.,* by the God who bore it. Individuals could not be reconciled to a holy God until He thus reconciled the world. Not until sin had been brought to do its very worst, and had in that culminating act been foiled, judged, and overcome; not till then could individuals receive the reconciliation. That was the unitary reconciliation they must receive in detail. God there, in a racial holiness amid racial curse, sets up a racial salvation, which our souls enter upon by faith. It is by Himself in His changeless love and pity that it is set up. It is not the Son's suffering and death, but His holy obedience to both that is the satisfying thing to God, the holiness of God the Son. In a sense, a great solemn sense, it is an exercise of God's absolute self-satisfaction, exhibited after a long historic process, amidst the dissatisfaction of a world's ruin. "In His love and in His pity He redeemed them." He set up reconciliation by an act of judgment on His Son, cutting off His own right hand that we might enter into the Kingdom of heaven: "In His love and in His pity He redeemed them; and He bare them, and carried them all the days of old." The redemption was a thing that was coming through the whole of Israel's history, and in a remoter sense through the whole history of the world. The changeless holiness must assert itself in such judgment as surely as in the kingdom. You all believe that the holiness of God must assert itself in the Kingdom of God. But how can there be a final kingdom without final judgment? Is not all judgment in the name of the king, even in our human society? Are not king and judge inseparable, as inseparable as king and father? We say today that king and father are inseparable. But king and judge are equally inseparable, especially if you take the great Old Testament idea. Christ submitted with all His heart to God's holy final judgment on the race. He did not view it as an unfortunate incident in His life. He did not treat it as though it happened to drop upon Him. But He treated it as the grand will of God, as the effectuation in history of God's holiness, which holiness must have complete response and practical confession both on its negative side of judgment and its positive side of obedience. Christ's death was atoning not simply because it was sacrifice even unto death, but because it was sacrifice unto holy and radical judgment. There is something much more than being obedient unto death. Plenty of men can be obedient unto death; but the core of Christianity is Christ's being obedient unto judgment, and unto the final judgment of holiness. It is being obedient to a kind of death prescribed by God, indispensable to the holiness of God's love, necessitated in such a world by the last moral conditions, and not simply inflicted by the wickedness of men.

Get rid of the idea that judgment is chiefly retribution, and directly infliction. Realize that it is, positively, the establishing and the securing of eternal righteousness and holiness. View punishment as an indirect and collateral necessity, like the surgical pains that make room for nature's curing power. You will then find nothing morally repulsive in the idea of judgment effected in and on Christ, any more than in the thought that the kingdom was set up in Him.

To conclude, then, God could only justify man before Him by justifying Himself and His holy law before men. If He had not vindicated His holiness to the uttermost in that way of judgment, it would not be a kind of holiness that men could trust. Thus a faith which could justify man, which could make a foundation for a new humanity, could not exist. We can only be eternally justified by faith in a God who justifies Himself as so holy that He must set up His holiness in human history at any price, even at the price of His own beloved and eternal Son.

I close, then, upon that unchangeable word of God's self-justifying holiness. Even the sinner could not trust a love that could not justify itself as holy. It is the holiness in God's love, I urge, that alone enables us to trust Him. Without that we should only love Him, and the love would fluctuate. For we could not be perfectly sure that His would not. It is the holiness in God's love that is the eternal, stable, unchangeable element in it - the holiness secured for history and its destine in the Cross. It is only the unchangeable that we could trust; and there alone we find it. If we only loved the love of God, we should have no stable, eternal, universal religion. But we love the *holy* love He established in Christ, and therefore we are safe with an everlasting salvation.

V. The Cross The Great Confessional

In the days of our fathers Christian belief was more solid within the Church than it is now; and the defending and expounding of Christianity, more especially the defending of it, had to concern itself with outsiders - outside the Church, and outside Christianity very often. Today our difficulties have changed; and a great part of our exposition must keep in view the fact that some of the most dangerous challenges of Christianity are found amongst those who claim the Christian name. There are those who have a very real reverence for the character of Jesus Christ, and they can speak, and do speak, quite sincerely, with great devotion and warmth and beauty, about Christ, and about many of the ideas that are associated with apostolic Christianity. All the same, they are strongly and sometimes even violently, antagonistic to that redemption which is the very center of the Christian faith; and they make denials and challenges which are bound to tell upon the existence of that faith before many generations are over. We do not take the true measure of the situation unless we realize that the thing which is at stake at this moment is something that will not affect the present generation, but is sure to affect two or three generations hence. Those who are concerned about Christianity on the largest scale today are concerned with what may be its position and its prospects then. The ideas at the center of the Christian faith are too large, too deep and subtle, to show their effects in one age; and the challenge of them does not show its effect in one generation or even in two. Individuals, society, and the Church, indeed, are able to go on, externally almost unaffected, by the way that they have upon them from the past; and it is only within the range of several generations that the destruction of truths with such a comprehensive range as those of Christianity takes effect. Therefore it is part of the duty of the Church, in certain sections and on certain occasions, to be less concerned about the effect of the Gospel upon the individual immediately, or on the present age, and to look ahead to what may be the result of certain changes in the future. God sets watchmen in Zion who have to keep their eye on the horizon; and it is only a drunken army that could scout their warning. We are not only bound to attend to the needs and interests of the present generation; we are trustees for a long future, as well as a long past. Therefore it is quite necessary that the Church should give very particular attention to these central and fundamental points whose influence, perhaps, is not so promptly prized, and whose destruction would not be so mightily felt at once, but would certainly become apparent in the days and decades ahead.

That is why one feels bound to invite attention, and to press attention, upon points concerning which it may very easily be said, "These are matters that do not concern my faith and my piety; I can afford to let these things alone." Perhaps A, B, and C can, and X, Y, and Z can; but the Christian Church cannot afford to let these things alone. The Church carries the individual amid much failure of his faith; there is a vicarious faith; but what is to carry the Church if its faith fail? Remove concern from these things, and the effect of the collective message of the Church to the great world becomes undermined. Then the world must look somewhere else than to the Church for that which is to save it. That is some apology for dwelling upon points which many people would say were simply theological and were outside the interest of the individual Christian. Theology simply means thinking in centuries. Religion tells on the present, but theology tells on the religion of the future and the race.

Moreover, there are always natures among Christian people who refuse, and properly refuse, to remain satisfied with superficial experiences or current views of their faith. They are bound by the spirit that moves within them - by the kind of temperament God has given them they are bound to penetrate to the heart, to the depths of things. Their work does not immediately pay; and while they grind in their mill the Philistines mock and the libertines jeer. But it would be a great misfortune if the whole of the work of the Church were measured by the standard which is so necessary in the world - the standard of what will immediately pay, or promptly tell. It is, of course, a great thing to go back upon the history of Christianity, and to point out to ourselves and to our people the great things that Christianity has done in the course of history. But you cannot rest Christianity upon that. You can only rest Christianity upon Christ Himself, and His living presence in the New Humanity. You can put the matter in this way. You can ask, On what did the Christianity rest of those who believed in the very first years of the Church's life? They had no results of Christianity before them. They had no history of the Church before them. They had not the glorious story of Christian philanthropy before them, nor the magnificent expansion of Christian doctrine, nor the enormous influence of the Christian Church and its effect upon the course of the world's history. On what did they rest their faith? That upon which they rested their faith must be that upon which we rest our faith when we come to a real crisis, and are driven into a real corner. It thus becomes necessary to go into the deep things of God as they are revealed to us by the Holy Spirit, through His inspired apostles, in Christ and His Cross.

From what I have said you will be prepared to hear me state that reconciliation is effected by the representative sacrifice of Christ crucified; by Christ crucified as the representative of God on the one hand and of Humanity, or the Church, on the other hand. Also it was by Christ crucified in connection with the divine judgment. Judgment is a far greater idea than sacrifice. For you see great sacrifices made for silly or mischievous causes, sacrifices which show no insight whatever into the moral order or the divine sanctity. Now this sacrifice of Christ, when you connect it with the idea of judgment, must in some form or other be described as a penal sacrifice. Round that word penal there rages a great deal of controversy. And I am using the word with some reserve, because there are forms of interpreting it which do the idea injustice. The sacrifice of Christ was a penal sacrifice. In what sense is that so? We can begin by clearing the ground, by asking, In what sense is it not true that the sacrifice of Christ was penal? Well, it cannot be true in the sense that God punished Christ. That is an absolutely unthinkable thing. How could God punish Him in whom He was always well pleased? The two things are a contradiction in terms. And it cannot be true in the sense that Christ was in our stead in such a way as to exclude and exempt us. The sacrifice of Christ, then, was penal not in the sense of God so punishing Christ that there is left us only religious enjoyment, but in this sense. There is a penalty and curse for sin; and Christ consented to enter that region. Christ entered voluntarily into the pain and horror which is sin's penalty from God. Christ, by the deep intimacy of His sympathy with men, entered deeply into the blight and judgment which was entailed by man's sin and which must be entailed by man's sin if God is a holy and therefore a judging God. It is impossible for us to say that God was angry with Christ; but still Christ entered the wrath of God, understanding that phrase as I endeavoured to explain it yesterday. He entered the penumbra of judgment, and from it He confessed in free action, He praised and justified by act, before the world, and on the scale of all the world, the holiness of God. You can therefore say that although Christ was not punished by God, He bore God's penalty upon sin. That penalty was not lifted even when the Son of God passed through. Is there not a real distinction between the two statements? To say that Christ was punished by God who was always well pleased with Him is an outrageous thing. Calvin himself repudiates the idea. But we may say that Christ did, at the depth of that great act of self-identification with us when He became man, He did enter the sphere of sin's penalty and the horror of sin's curse, in order that, from the very midst and depth of it, His confession and praise of God's holiness might rise like a spring of fresh water at the bottom of the bitter sea, and sweeten all. He justified God in His judgment and wrath. He justified God in this thing.

So the act of Christ had this twofold aspect. On the one hand it was God offering, and on the other hand it was man confessing. Now, what was it that Christ chiefly confessed? I hope you have read McLeod Campbell on the Atonement. Every minister ought to know that book, and know it well. But there is one criticism to be made upon the great, fine, holy book. And it is this. It speaks too much, perhaps, about Christ confessing human sin, about Christ becoming the Priest and Confessor before God of human sin and exposing it to God's judgment. The horror of the Cross expresses the repentance of the race before a holy God for its sin. But considerable difficulties arise in that connection, and critics were not slow to point them out. How could Christ in any real sense confess a sin, even a racial sin, with whose guilt He had nothing in common? Now that is rather a serious criticism if the confession of sin were the first charge upon either Christ or us, if the confession of human sin were the chief thing that God wanted or Christ did I think it is certainly a defect in that great book that it fixes our attention too much upon Christ's vicarious confession *of human sin.* The same criticism applies to another very fine book, that by the late Canon Moberly, or Christ Church, "Atonement and Personality." I once had the privilege of meeting Canon Moberly in discussion on this subject, and ventured to point out that defect in his theory, and I was relieved to find that on the occasion the same criticism was also made by Bishop Gore. But we get out of the difficulty, in part at least, if we recognize that the great work of Christ, while certainly it did confess human sin, was yet not to confess that, but to confess something greater, namely God's holiness in His judgment upon sin. His confession, indeed, was not in so many words, but in a far more mighty way, by act and deed of life and death. The great confession is not by word of mouth - it is by the life, in the sense, not of mere conduct, but in the great personal sense in which life contains conduct and transcends death. Christ confessed not merely human sin - which in a certain sense, indeed, He could not do - but He confessed God's holiness in reacting mortally against human sin, in cursing human sin, in judging it to its very death. He stood in the midst of human sin full of love to man, such love as enabled Him to identify Himself in the most profound, sympathetic way with the evil race; fuller still of love to the God whose name He was hallowing; and, as with one mouth, as if the whole race confessed through Him, as with one soul, as though the whole race at last did justice to God through His soul, He lifted up His face unto God and said, "Thou art holy in all Thy judgments, even in this judgment which turns not aside even from Me, but strikes the sinful spot if even I stand on it." The dereliction upon the Cross, the sense of love's desertion by love, was Christ's practical confession of the holy God's repulsion of sin. He accepted the divine situation - the situation of the race before God. By God's will He did so. By His own free consent He did so. Remember the distinction between God's changeless love and God's varying treatment of the soul. God made Him sin, treated Him as if He were sin; He did not view Him as sinful. That is quite another matter. God made Him to be sin - it does not say He made Him sinful. God lovingly treated Him as human sin, and with His consent judged human sin in Him and on Him. Personal guilt Christ could never confess. There is that in guilt which can only be confessed by the guilty. "I did it." That kind of confession Christ could never make. That is the part of the confession that we make, and we cannot make it effectually until we are in union with Christ and His great lone work of perfectly and practically confessing the holiness of God. There is a racial confession that can only be made by the holy; and there is a personal confession that can only be made by the guilty. That latter, I say, is a confession Christ could never make. In that respect Christ did not die, and did not suffer, did not confess, in our stead. We alone, the guilty, can make that confession; but we cannot make it with Christian effect without the Cross and the confession there. We say then not only "I did this," but "I am guilty before the holiness confessed in the Cross." The grand sin is not to sin against the law but against the Cross. The sin of sins is not transgression, but unfaith.

So also of holiness, there is a confession of holiness which can only be made by God, the Holy. If God's holiness was to be fully confessed, in act and deed, in life, and death, and love transcending both, it can only be done by Godhead itself.

Therefore we press the words to their fullness of meaning: "God was in Christ reconciling," not reconciling through Christ, but actually present as Christ reconciling, doing in Christ His own work of reconciliation. It was done by Godhead itself, and not by the Son alone. The old theologians were right when they insisted that the work of redemption was the work of the whole Trinity - Father, Son, and Holy Spirit; as we express it when we baptize into the new life of reconcilement in the threefold name. The holiness of God was confessed in man by Christ, and this holy confession of Christ's is the source of the truest confession of our sin that we can make. Our saving confession is not merely "I did so and so," but "I did it against a holy, saving God." "I have sinned against heaven and in thy sight," sinned before infinite holiness and forgiving grace. God could not forgive until man confessed, and confessed not only his own sin but confessed still more - God's holiness in the judgment of sin. The confession also had to be made in life and action, as the sin was done. That is to say, it had to be made religiously and not theologically, by an experience and not an utterance. A verbal confession, however sincere, could not fully own an actual sin. If we sin by deed we must so confess. It is made thus religiously, spiritually, experimentally, practically by Jesus Christ's life, its crown of death, and His life eternal. The more sinful man is, the less can he thus confess either his own sin or God's holiness. Therefore God did it in man by a love which was as great as it was holy, by an infinite love. That is to say, by a love which was as closely and sympathetically identified with man as it was identified with the power of the holy God.

So we have arrived at this. The great confession was made not alone in the precise hour of Christ's death, although it was consummated there. It had to be made in life and act, and not in a mere feeling or statement; and for this purpose death must be organically one with the whole life. You cannot sever the death of Christ from the life of Christ. When you think of the self-emptying which brought Christ to earth, His whole life here was a living death. The death of Christ must be organic with His whole personal life and action. And that means not only His earthly life previous to the Cross, but His whole celestial life from the beginning, and to this hour, and to all eternity. The death of Christ is the central point of eternity as well as of human history. His own eternal life revolves on it. And we shall never be so good and holy at any point, even in eternity, that we shall not look into the Cross of Christ as the center of all our hope in earth or heaven. It is Christ that works out His own redemption and reconciliation, from God's right hand, throughout the course of history. I would gather that up in one phrase. Christ is the perpetual providence of His own salvation. Christ, acting through His Spirit, is the eternal providence of His own salvation. The apostles never separated reconciliation in any age from the Cross and blood of Jesus Christ. If ever we do that (and many are doing it today) we throw the New Testament overboard. The bane of so much that claims to be more spiritual religion at the present day is that it simply jettisons the New Testament, and with it historic Christianity. The extreme critics, people that live upon monism and immanence, rationalist religion and spiritual impressionism, are people who are deliberately throwing overboard the New Testament as a whole, deeply as they prize it in parts. They say that the apostolic views and interpretations of Christ's work may have been all very well for people who knew no better than men did at so early a period, but we are now a long way beyond that, and we must re-edit the New Testament theology, especially as to Christ's death. I keep urging, whatever we do let us do it frankly, let us do it with our eyes open and with eyes competent to take the measure of what we are doing. The trying thing is that tremendous renunciations should be blandly made, without, apparently, any sense of their appalling dimensions, and of the huge thing that is being so ignorantly done. (See note at the end of this lecture.)

The apostles, I say, never separated reconciliation from the Cross and the blood of Jesus Christ. The historic Church has never done so, with all its divisions. And what the Cross meant for the apostles as Jews, with their history and education, was something like this. If you go back to the Old Testament, you find that the whole kingdom of God and destiny of man turns on the treatment of sin. And either the sin was atoned or the sinner was punished. But there were some sins that never could be atoned for, what are described as sins with a high hand, presumptuous sins, deliberate, defiant sins, as distinct from sins of ignorance or weakness, when a man so identified himself with his sin that he became inseparable from it. The man guilty of them was put outside the camp, his communication was cut with the saved community of Israel. He was committed to the outer darkness. There remained only punishment and death. The punishment was expulsion from the covenant, and so from life. And as there is little about immortality in the Old Testament, it was death for good and all. But in the Cross of Christ there is no sin excluded from atonement. I know of course what you are thinking about - the sin against the Holy Ghost. That is far too large a subject to enter on. I can only say that I am not keeping it out of my survey. And I repeat, there is no sin excluded from atonement. Death as punishment of sin was absorbed in Christ's sacrifice. Such was its atoning work that the judgment due to all mankind was absorbed, and the sin of sins now was fixed refusal of that Grace. The Cross bought up all other debts, so to say.

To return to my old point. The objection to speaking of Christ's death as penalty is two-fold. God could not punish One with whom He was always well pleased. Consequently Christ could not suffer punishment in the true sense of the word without having a guilty conscience. If the bearing of punishment were the whole of Christ's work, there was something in that way which He did not and could not do - He could not bear the penalty of remorse. But the whole of His work, was not the bearing of punishment; it was not the acceptance of suffering. It was the recognition and justification of it, the "homologation" of God's judgment and God's holiness in it.

The death and suffering of Christ was something very much more than suffering - it was atoning action. At various stages in the history of the Church - not the Roman Catholic Church only but Protestantism also - exaggerated stress has been laid upon the sufferings of Christ. But it is not a case of what He suffered but what He did. Christ's suffering was so divine a thing because He freely transmitted it into a great act. It was suffering accepted and transfigured by holy obedience under the conditions of curse and blight which sin and brought upon man according to the holiness of God. The suffering was a sacrifice to God's holiness. In so far it was penalty. But the atoning thing was not its amount or acuteness, but its obedience, its sanctity.

There are pathetic ways of thinking about Christ regard Him too much as a mere individual before God. They do not satisfy if Christ's relation with man was a racial one and He represented Humanity. Especially they do not hold good if that relationship was no mere blood relationship, natural relationship, but a supernatural relationship - blood relationship only in the mystic Christian sense. We are blood relations of Christ, but not in the natural sense of that term, only in the supernatural sense, as those who are related to Him in His blood, in His death, and in His Spirit. The value of Christ's unity and sympathy with us was not simply that He was continuous with the race at its head. It was not a relation of *identity*. The race was not prolonged into Him. The value consists in that life-act of *self-identification* by which Christ the eternal Son of God became man. We hear much about Christ's essential identity with the human race. That is not true in the sense in which other great men, like Shakespeare, for instance, were identical with the human race, gathering up in consummation its natural genius. Christ's identity was not natural or created identity, but the self-identification of the Creator. Everything turns upon this - whether Christ was a created being, however grand, or whether He was of increate Godhead.

As Head of the human race by this voluntary self-identification with it, Christ took the curse and judgment, which did not belong to Himself as sinless. And what He owned was not so much the depth of our misery as the depth of our guilt; and He did it sympathetically, by the moral sympathy possible only to the holy. Nor did He simply take the full measure of our guilt. His owning it means very much more than that His moral perceptions were so deep and piercing that He could measure our guilt as a bystander of acute moral penetration could. He carried it in His own moral experience as only divine sympathy could. And in dumb action He spread it out as it is before God. He felt sin and its horror as only the holy could as God did. We learn in our measure to do that when we escape from the indifference of our egotism and come under His Cross and near His heart; we learn to do as Christ did as we enter into living union with Christ. And we then rise above purity - for purity is only shamed by sin - we rise to holiness, which is burdened with sin and all its load. How much more than pure Christ was! How much fuller of meaning is such a word as "holy" or "holiness" than either "pure" or "purity". Purity is shamed by human sin. Holiness carries it as a load, and carries it to its destruction. In the great desertion Christ could not feel Himself a sinner whom God rejects. For the sinner cannot carry sin; he collapses under it. Christ felt Himself treated as the sin which God Recognizes and repels by His very holiness. It covered and hid Him from God. He was made sin (not sinful, as I say). The holiness of God becomes our salvation not by slackness of demand but by completeness of judgment; not because He relaxes His demand, not because He spends less condemnation on sin, lets us off or lets sin off, or lets Christ off ("spared not"); but because in Christ judgment becomes finished and final, because none but a holy Christ could spread sin out in all its sinfulness for thorough judgment. I have a way of putting it which startles some of my friends. The last judgment is past. It took place on Christ's Cross. What we talk about as the last judgment is simply the working out of Christ's Cross in detail. The final judgment, the absolute judgment, the crucial judgment for the race took place in principle on the Cross of Christ. Sin has been judged finally there. All judgment is given to the Son in virtue of His Cross. All other debts are bought up there.

It is not simply that in the Cross of Christ all punishment was shown to be corrective. A favorite theme on the part of many of those who challenge the apostolic position about the death of Christ is that it was only the crowning exposition of the great principle that all punishment is really corrective and education. We cannot say that. There is plenty of punishment that hardens and hardens. That is why we are obliged to leave such questions as universal restoration unsolved. Even when we recognize the absolute power of God's salvation, we also recognize that it is in the power of the human soul to harden itself until it become shrunk into such a tough and irreducible mass as it seems the very grace of God could do nothing with. Certainly there are people here, in this life, who become so tough in their sin that the grace of God is in vain. And I am not sure that among those who are toughest are not some who are much comforted by their religion. You can do something with a hardened sinner. He can be broken to pieces. But I do not know what you can do with a viscous saint, with those who are wrapped in the wool, soaked in the comfort of their religion, and tanned to leather, soft and tough as a glove, by its bitterest baptisms. I once used an expression of these people which was somewhat criticized. I called them "moral tabbies." Is there anything more comfortable, and selfish, and hopeless than a really accomplished tabby? When religion becomes perverted to be a means of mere comfort and dense self-satisfaction, it becomes an integument so tough that even the grace of God cannot get through it, or a substance so flaccid that it cannot be handled.

I find it convenient, you observe, to distinguish between punishment and penalty. A man who loses his life in the fire-damp, where he is looking for the victims of an accident, pays the penalty of sacrifice, but he does not receive its punishment. And I think it useful to speak of Christ as taking the penalty of sin, while I refuse to speak of His taking its punishment. I would avoid every word that would suggest that He was punished in connection with His salvation. It robs the whole act of ethical value to say so. Penalty is made to honor God in the Cross of Christ, and thus it becomes a blessing to us. Not that our punishment is turned to good account in its subjective results upon us, but that Christ's judgment has objective value to the honor of God's holiness. He turned the penalty He endured into sacrifice He offered. And the sacrifice He offered was the judgment He accepted. His passive suffering became active obedience, and obedience to a holy doom. He did not steel His face to the suffering He had to endure, as though it were a fate to which He had to set His teeth and go through it in a stoic way. He never regarded it as a mere infliction. For Him, whoever inflicted it, it was the holiest thing in all the world - it was the will and judgment of God. All the Old Testament told Him that the Kingdom of God could never come without the prior judgment of God; and He was prepared to force that judgment in His impatience for the Kingdom. * He answered the judgment of God with a grand affirmative act. The willing acceptance of final judgment was for Jesus the means presented by God for effecting human reconciliation and the Divine Kingdom. The essence of all sacrifice, which is self-surrender to God, was lifted out of the Old Testament garb of symbolism, and was made a moral reality in Christ's holy obedience. In the Old Testament we have the lamb and the various other things brought for offering; but where did their essential value lie? In the obedience of the offerer; in the fact that those institutions were given and prescribed by holy God, however their details were due to man. And the presentation of the victim was valuable, not because of anything in the victim, but because of the obedience and surrender of the will with which the offerer presented it. This is the bearing of sin - the holy bearing of its judgment. This is the taking of sin away - the acknowledgment of judgment as holy, wise, and good, and its conversion into blessing; the absorption and conversion of judgment into confession and praise, the removal of that guilt which stood between God and man's reconciliation - the robbing sin of its power to prevent communion with God.

I should, therefore, express the difference between the old view and the new by saying that one emphasizes substitutionary expiation and the other emphasizes solidary reparation, consisting of due acknowledgment of God's holiness, and the honoring of that and not of His honor.

Now let me pass as I close today to two or three points I want specially to emphasize.

There is one quotation which I wanted to make at a particular point and did not. The Reformers are still on the whole, the maters of the great verities of experience in connection with the work of Christ. They had an amazing insight into the morbid psychology of the conscience. They did understand what sin meant, and they said this - the sinner, beginning with indifference, must keep flying from God until he actually hate God as a persecutor, unless he grasp the pursuit as God's mercy. Indifference could not stop at indifference, but goes on through aversion to hate. Even if a man die indifferent in this life, he comes into circumstances where he ceases to be indifferent. If we believe about a future at all, it will be impossible for an indifferent man to remain indifferent when he has passed on there. Indifference is an unstable position. It changes either upward or downward - downward into antagonism, into deadly hate against God, something Satanic; or upwards it passes into acceptance of God's mercy by faith, and all its blossom and fruit, its joy and peace in the Holy Ghost. The Reformers were perfectly right. It is only our dull experience and preoccupied vision which prevent us seeing that it is so.

Then I should like to call attention to this value in such a cross. It is only the judgment sacrifice of the Son of God that assures the sinner of the deep changelessness of grace. Forgiving is not forgetting. Popular theology too often tends to pacify us by reducing the offense. But the Reformers put the matter quite otherwise in saying that a justifying faith only goes with a full sense of guilt. You cannot get a full, justifying faith without a full sense and confession of guilt. We always have mistrust in the background of our own self-extenuations. When conscience begins to work and you begin to extenuate, when you try your hand earnestly at justifying yourself to yourself, you have some idea of how much more vast must be God's justification of you before Himself. You cannot cease to ask what charge conscience has against you. Then you magnify that to God's charge. If your heart condemn you, His condemnation is greater than that of your condemning heart. Do you consider His conscience? His conscience has to be pacified as well as His heart indulged. And if His conscience be not met, ours is not sure. Has His conscience been met? Conscience has always mistrust in the background if grace is mere remission. Mere remission of sin does not satisfy even us. If conscience witnesses, against our extenuations, to the holy majesty of moral claim, is it to be less severe and less changeless than the claim of God Himself? Conscience has in trust God's law and its majesty, which must be made good, as mere remission does not make it. Suppose I transgress and I hear the message of grace, does it tell me the accusing, irrepressible demand of conscience, the haunting fear of judgment, was an illusion? It is doing me very ill service if it does. True, there is now no condemnation for faith; but if the message of grace ever teaches us that the judgment of conscience is exaggeration, is illusion, it is not the true grace of God. If a message of grace tell us there was and is no judgment any more, and that God has simply put judgment on one side and has not exercised it, that cannot be the true grace of God. Surely the grace of God cannot stultify our human conscience like that! So we are haunted by mistrust, unless conscience be drowned in a haze of heart. We have always the feeling and fear that there is judgment to follow. How may I be sure that I may take the grace of God seriously and finally, how be sure that I have complete salvation, that I may entirely trust it through the worst my conscience may say? Only thus, that God is the Reconciler, that He reconciles in Christ's Cross that the judgment of sin was there for good and all. We are judged now by the Cross, and by the Cross we stand or fall. The great sin is not something we do, but it is refusing to make ourselves right with God in Christ's Cross. We are judged in the end by our relation to the Cross of Christ. It is the principle of our moral world. All judgment is committed to that Son. We stand before God at last according as we are owned by Christ. We are confessed by Him according to our confession of Him. Nemesis on us is hallowed as a part of the judgment on Him to whose death we are joined. There is no such thorough assertion of God's holy, loving law anywhere as there, where in the Cross it was given its own, and was perfected in judgment in Him who became a curse for us. His prayer for His murderers, or the closing sigh of victory in the midst of that judgment, vouches for ever to this, that it is the same holy will which judges man's wickedness and also loves us and gives His Son for a propitiation for us. Only that holiness which is changeless in its judgment could be changeless also in grace. His grace was so little to be foiled that He graciously took His own judgment. Thus the severity of conscience becomes the certainty of salvation.

But changeless in judgment! Does that mean exacting the uttermost farthing of penalty, of suffering? Does it mean that in the hour of His death Christ suffered, compressed into one brief moment, all the pains of hell which the human race deserved. We cannot think about things in that way. God does not work by such equivalents. What is required is not an equivalent penalty, but an adequate confession of His holiness. Let us get rid of that materialist idea of equivalents. What Christ gave to God was not an equivalent penalty, but an adequate confession of God's holiness, rising from amid extreme conditions of sin. God's holiness, then, was so little to be mocked, that He actually took His own judgment to save it. He spared not His own Son - His own self. His severity of conscience becomes at the same moment our security of salvation. And the more conscience preaches the changelessness of the judging God, the more it preaches the same changelessness in the grace of Christ.

There is another consequence. Only the eternal Reconciler, the High Priest, can guarantee us our full redemption. "Take, my soul, thy full salvation." You cannot do it except you do it in such a Cross. It is not enough to have in the Cross a great demonstration of God's love, a forgiveness of the past which leaves us to fend for ourselves in the future Is my moral power so great after all, then, that, supposing I believe past things were settled in Christ's Cross, I may now feel I can run in my own strength? Can I be perfectly confident about meeting temptation? Nay, we must depend daily upon the continued energy of the crucified and risen One. We must depend daily upon the action of that same Christ whose action culminated there but did not end there. His death is as organic with His heavenly life as it was with His earthly. What is the meaning of His perpetual intercession if it does not mean that - the exhausted energy of His saving act? It is by His work from heaven that we appropriate His work upon earth. He guarantees our perfection as well as our redemption.

The last step. It is only the atoning reconciliation of a whole world that guarantees the final perfecting of that world by its Creator. How do we know that creation is going to be perfected? How do we know that it is to be to the glory of God who made it and called it good? How do we know the world will not be a failure for God with all but the group of people saved in an ark of some kind? We only know because we believe in the reconciliation of the whole world in Christ's Cross. There is a great deal of pessimism today, much doubt as to whether perfection really remains for the whole world; and you find people in the burdened West drawn to the Buddhistic idea of the human soul's extinction. Some Christians content themselves with individual salvation out of a world which is left in the lurch, or they are satisfied with personal union with Christ securing their own future. But the gospel deals with the world of men as a whole. It argues the restoration of all things, a new heaven and a new earth. It intends the regeneration of human society as a whole. Christ is the Savior of the world, who was also the agent of its creation. The Creator has not let His world get out of hand for good and all. That is to say, our faith is social and communal in its nature. We must have a social gospel. And this you cannot get upon the basis of mere individual or sectional salvation. You can only have a social gospel upon one basis, namely, that Christ saved, reconciled the whole world as a unity, the whole of society and history. The Object of our faith, Jesus Christ, is what our fathers used to call a federal Person, a federal Savior, in a federal act. All humanity is in Him and in His act. It is quite true every man must believe for himself, but no man can believe by himself or unto himself. The Christian faith fades away if it is not nourished and built up in a community, in a Church. And the Church fades away if it do not hold this faith in trust for the whole world. Each one of us is saved only by the act and by the Person that saved the whole world.

* See Schweitzer's very remarkable "Quest of the Historical Jesus" (A. and C. Black) - the last two chapters - where a dogmatic and atoning motive in Jesus is declared by an advanced critic to have been the explanation of His death.

VI. The Precise Problem Today *

There is a popular impression about both philosophy and theology that the history of their problems is very sterile; that it is not a long development, carrying the discussion on with growing insight from age to age, and passing from thinker to thinker with growing depth, but rather a scene in which each newcomer demolishes the work of his predecessor in order to put in its place some theory doomed in turn to the same fruitless fate. Truly, as Hegel says, if that were so with philosophy, its history would become one of the saddest and sorriest things, and it would have no right to go on. And if it were so with theology, we should not only be distressed for Humanity, but we should be skeptical about the Holy Spirit in the Church. It could be the Church of no Holy Spirit if those who translated its life into thought did not offer to posterity a spectacle higher than dragons that tare each other in the slime, or lions that bit and devoured one another.

As a matter of truth and fact, both philosophy and theology have not only a chronicle but a history. They register the highest spiritual evolution of the race. The wave behind rolls on the wave before. The past is not devoured but lives on, and comes to itself in the future. The new arrivals do not consume their predecessors, and do not ignore them; they interpret them and carry them forwards. They take their fertile place in the great organic movement. They modulate what is behind upwards into what is to come. They correct the past and enrich it; and they hand on their corrected past to be a foundation for the workers yet to be.

The amateur, or the self-taught, therefore is at a great disadvantage. He does not take up the problem where the scientific succession laid it down. He does not come in where his great co-workers left off. He must start *ab ovo*. He must do over again for himself what they have conspired to do better. He risks "being a fool at first hand." He wants himself criticizing what has long been dropped, and slaying the long-time slain. He throws away effort in establishing what the competent have agreed to accept. And he misses the right points to attack or to strengthen, because he has not surveyed the ground. Every now and then one meets the capable amateur, whose misfortune it has been to have no schooling in the scientific history or method of the subject, who applied to it a shrewd mother-wit or an earnest but uninstructed conscience, and who perhaps publishes a theory of Incarnation or Atonement which, for all its hints and glimpses of truth, makes no real contribution either to the history or the merits of the case. This is the misfortune of the self-taught who goes straight to his Bible for the materials of his theology, and ignores most of the treatment the problem has received from the greatest minds in the history of the Church or the soul. The Bible is enough for our saving faith, but it is not enough for our scientific theology.

To make the most therefore of godly and able men, who would else be wasted more or less, it is well that we should teach them at the outset to take up the question where they find it, to begin where their best predecessors left off, to work upon results, and to carry forward the subject in the train of its evolution from the great and growing past. Let us couple up with the past, and repay its gifts by fructifying them for the future. Let us call in our thought, and concentrate it upon the precise question which previous thinkers have left us to solve.

There is, thus, another thing we have to do. We have to try to find a due place for those views which, however one-sided, yet do compel attention to aspects that the Church from time to time ignores. We have to meet, satisfy, and exceed such views. Much, for instance, has been done in the lifetime of most of us to correct and extend those views of Christ's work which were so rigidly objective that they became external. It has been urged that the Church long thought too much of Christ's action on God and not enough of His action on man. And what is called the moral theory of the Atonement has therefore been pressed upon us, to replace the ultra-objective and satisfactionary view. And the pressure has often been so hard that an objective theory has been entirely denied as immoral, and denied sometimes with a scorn unjustified by either the mental acumen or moral dignity of the critic.

But in spite of this over-pressure, and the occasional insolence that goes with ignorance, it remains our duty to find a proper place in our view of the whole great subject for that effect of Christ upon men which has meant so much of the sanctity of the Church. We have to meet, satisfy, and transcend those pleas which have been called into existence to redress the balance of theological neglect, and to fill out that which was behind in our grasp of the manifold work. Especially we have to adjust our theology of Christ's work to those who observe that the repentance of the guilty is an essential condition of forgiveness, and who go on to ask how we can speak of a finished reconciliation or atonement by a sinless Christ, who could not possibly present before God a repentance of that kind.

There are certain results which, it may be said, we have definitely reached in correction of what has long been known as the popular view of Christ's death and work. They are modern, and they owe much to Schleiermacher, Ritschl, McLeod Campbell, Maurice and others; but they have also been shown to be scriptural, by a new, objective and scientific investigation of what the Bible has to say on the subject. When we have brought the long history of the question up to date, balanced the books, and taken account of the general agreement on the modern side, we can then go on to ask where exactly the question now stands.

The modifications on which the best authorities are substantially at one we have seen to be such as these: -

1. Reconciliation is not the result of a change in God from wrath to love. It flows from the changeless will of a loving God. No other view could make the reconciliation sure. If God changed *to* it, He might change *from* it. And the sheet-anchor of the soul for Eternity would then have gone by the board. Forgiveness arose at no point in time. Grace was there before even creation. It abounded before sin did. The holiness which makes sin sin, is one with the necessity to destroy sin in gracious love.

2. Reconciliation rests on Christ's person, and it is effected by His entire work, doing, and suffering. This work does three things. (1) It reveals and puts into historic action the changeless grace of God. (2) It reveals and establishes His holiness, and therein also the sinfulness of sin. And (3) it exhibits a Humanity in perfect tune with that will of God. And it does more than exhibit these things - it *sets them up,* grace, holiness, and the new Humanity in its Head.

3. This reconciling and redeeming work of Christ culminates in His suffering unto death, which is indeed more of an act than an experience. Here, in the Cross, is the summit of His revelation of grace, of sin, and of Humanity. And the central feature of this threefold revelation in the Cross is the holiness of God's love. It is this holiness that deepens error into sin, sin into guilt, and guilt into repentance; without which any sense of forgiveness would be but an anodyne and not a grace, a self-flattering unction to the soul and not the peace of God.

4. In this relation to God's holiness and its satisfaction, nobody now thinks of the transfer of our punishment to Christ in its entirety - including the worst pains of hell in a sense of guilt. Christ experienced the world's hate, and the curse of the Law in the sense of the suffering entailed on man by sin; but a direct infliction of men's total deserts upon Him by God is unthinkable. His penalty was not punishment, because it was dissociated from the sense of desert. Whatever we mean by atonement must be interpreted in that sense. And judgment is a much better word than either penalty or punishment.

5. What we have in Christ's work is not the mere pre-requisite or condition of reconciliation, but the actual and final effecting of it in principle. He was not making it possible, He was doing it. We are spiritually in a reconciled world, we are not merely in a world in process of empirical reconciliation. Our experience of religion is experience of a thing done once for all, for ever, and for the world. That is, it is more than even experience, it is a faith. The same act as put God's forgiveness on a moral foundation also revolutionized Humanity. Hence we are not disposed to speak of substitution ** so much as of representation. But it is representation by One who creates by His act the Humanity He represents, and does not merely sponsor it. *The same act* as disburdens us of guilt commits us to a new life. Our Savior in His salvation is not only our comfort but our power; not merely our rescuer but our new life. His work is in the same act reclamation as well as rescue.

6. Another thing may perhaps be taken as recognized in some form by the main line of judicious advance in our subject. The work of Christ was moral and not

official. It was the energy and victory of His own moral personality, and not simply the filling of a position, the discharge of an office He held. His victory was not due to His rank, but to His will and conscience. It lay in His faithfulness to the uttermost amid temptations morally real and psychologically relevant to what He was. It was a work that drew on His whole personality, and was built into the nature of that personality as a moral necessity of it. What He did He did not do simply in the room and stead of others, He did it as a necessity of His own person also - though its effect for them was not what it was for Him. He fulfilled an obligation under which His own personality lay; He did not simply pay the debts of other people. He fulfilled a personal vocation.

And His faithfulness was not only to a vocation. It was to a special vocation, that of a Redeemer, not merely a saint. The immediate source of His suffering was not the sight of human sin, and it was not a general holiness in Him. It was not the quivering of the saint's purity at the touch of evil. But it was the suffering of One who touched sin *as the Redeemer*. He would not have suffered for sin as He did, had He not faced it as its destroyer. Not only was this His vocation as a moral hero, but His special vocation as Savior. It was the work of a moral personality at the heart of the race, of One who concentrated on a special yet universal task - that of Redemption.

His perfection was not that of a paragon, one who could do better what every soul and genius of the race could do well. He was not all the powers and excellencies of mankind rolled into one superman. But His perfection was that of the race's Redeemer. It was interior to all other powers and achievements. It was central both for God and man. He made man's center and God's coincide. He took mankind at its enter and laid it on the center of God. His identification with man was not extensive but intensive, it was not discursive and parallel, so to say. It was morally central and creative. He was not Humanity on its divine side; He was its new life from the inside. The problem He had to solve was the supreme and central moral problem of guilt; and the work could only be done by the native action of a personality moral in its nature and methods, moral to the pitch of the Holy.

It is an immense gain thus to construe Christ's work as that of a moral personality instead of a heavenly functionary. It brings it into line with the modern mind and into organic union with the moral problem of the race. It enables us to realize that every step of the moral victory in His life was a step also in the Redemption of the whole human conscience. And we grasp with new power the idea that His crowning victory of the Cross was the victory in principle of the whole race in Him - that Justification is really one with Reconciliation, and what He did before God contained all He was to do on man. It makes possible for us what my last lecture will attempt to indicate - a unitary view of His whole work and person.

7. After these great modifications and gains, we have cleared the ground to ask with some exactness just where the question at the moment stands. What was the divinest thing, the atoning, satisfying thing, the thing offered to God, in Christ; the thing, therefore, final and precious in what He did? The permanent thing in

Christianity must be that which gives it its chief value to God. We are now beyond the crude alternative that so easily besets us, "Did Christ's work bear upon God or on man?" Neither alone would be true Reconciliation. Neither Orthodoxy nor Socinianism has it. But we have to ask this: "Can we combine the truth in each alternative? Can we reach the value of Christ's saving work to God (*i.e.* its true and final value) if we exclude its effect within man? Must we not take that in? *Nihil in effectu quod non prius in causa.* Must we not include the effect to get the full value of the cause, and give a full account of it?"

Now, let us own at the outset that the first things we must be sure about are the objective reality of our religion, its finality, and its initiative in God's free grace independent of act or desert of ours. But if we start there, it looks as if we were shut up to the first of the crude alternatives, as if the idea of Christ's work as acting on God only gave the best effect to these conditions. It looks as if the old theory alone guaranteed a salvation finished on the Cross, one wholly God's in His grace, one that ensures a full and objective release of the conscience. These things are not secured by what we do, but by Christ's work on the Cross. Moreover, that work was done for the whole of mankind, and was complete even for those who as yet make no response. And, besides, that first alternative is a view that seems to have the letter of Scripture with it. It does look as if we could not have full security except by trust of an objective something, done over our heads, and complete without any reference to our response or our despite.

But the difficulties begin when we ask what the objective something was. How describe it? For that purpose the old doctrine used juridical forms. But these are not large enough for the dimensions of a modern world, or for its deepened ethical insight. How exactly could the obedience of Christ stand for the obedience of all? It was the fulfilment of His own personal vocation; how does it stand for the obedience of every other person? Or how does the suffering of Christ restore the moral order, especially one He never broke? If you treat it as punishment, that punishment alone does not restore the moral order. And, if we say He did not do that, He did not restore a moral order, so much as acknowledge and confess the holiness of God in His judgment, is not the value of that recognition still greatly impaired by the fact that it is not made by the guilty but the Guiltless, who is not directly affected by the connection between sin and suffering. A finished religion would then be set up without the main thing - the acknowledgment by the guilty. That acknowledgment, that repentance, would then be outside the complete act, and would be at best but a sequel of it; whereas we ought to give a real place in a complete work of Reconciliation to our repentance (which some extremists say is all that is required), or to Christ's moral action on us. Do we not need to include in some way the effect in the cause, in order to give the cause its full and final value, *i.e.*, its value to God. The thing of price done by Christ for God, must it not already include the thing done upon men? Does not Christ's confession of God's holiness include man's confession of his sin?

Let us return to that idea of the moral order which is at the bottom of this objective theory. We ask whether the moral order is what the Bible means by the idea of the righteousness of God. The righteousness of God is not only holy but gracious, not only regulative and retributory, but also forgiving and restoring. It seems, indeed, in the Gospels to need no other condition of forgiveness than repentance. This is so; and it is all very well, we have seen, for individual cases. But we have to deal, as Christ at last had to deal, with the forgiveness of a world, the pardon of solidary sin. And we need to be sure, as Christ alone with His insight could be sure, that the repentance is true and deep. There it is that we are carried into questions which the Cross alone can answer. How shall I know how much repentance is deep enough? Where find a repentance wide enough to cover the sin of a guilty world? Could Christ offer that? No; directly, He could not. He could not offer it as a pathos, a personal experience, for He had no guilt. But, then, guilt is much more than a sense of guilt. And the essence of repentance is not its intensity or passion but the thing confessed. It is therefore the holiness more even than the sin that holiness makes so sinful. It is the due and understanding acknowledgment of the holiness offended. And this only a sinless Christ could really do, who was also sympathetic enough with men to do it from their side. And only the sinless could realize what sin meant for God.

Farther, this acknowledgment is not simply verbal, nor simply a matter of profound moral conviction and admission, but it must be a practical confession, as practical as the sin. It must place itself as if it were active sin under the reaction of the Divine holiness; it must be made sin. That is, it must accept judgment as the only adequate acknowledgment of the holy God in a sinful world; it must allow His holy law to assert itself in the Savior's person in the form forced on the sinner's Friend. He bore this curse as God's judgment, praised it, hallowed it, absorbed it; and His resurrection showed that He exhausted it.

But would His acceptance of judgment for us be possible, would it stand to our good, would it be of value in God's sight for us, if He were not in moral solidarity with us? How could it? What God sought was nothing so pagan as a mere victim outside our conscience and over our heads. It was a Confessor, a Priest, one taken from among men. But then this moral solidarity is the very thing that also gives, and must give, Him His mighty and revolutionary power on us. What makes it possible for Him to be a Divine victim or a Divine priest for us also makes Him a new Creator in us His offering of a holy obedience to God's judgment is therefore valuable to God for us which also makes Him such a moral power upon us and in us. His creative regenerative action on us is a part of that same moral solidarity which also makes His acceptance of judgment stand to our good, and His confession of God's holiness to be the ground of ours. The same stroke on the one Christ went upward to God's heart and downward to ours.

Is this not clear? Christ could make no due confession of holiness for us in judgment if He were outside Humanity, if He were a third party satisfying God over our head. The acknowledgment would not be really from the side of the culprit, certainly not from his interior, his conscience. The judgment would not really be the judgment of *our* sin, which would therefore be still due. To be of final value the atoning judgment must be also within the conscience of the guilty. But how is the judgment, the self-condemnation, the confession within our guilty conscience to be offered to God as an ingredient of Christ's reconciling work and not its mere sequel? It is not yet there. Or else it is nothing worth offering by way of atonement when it is there. Is there any way of offering our self-condemnation as a meritorious contribution to forgiveness? Can it be included in the Divine ground of forgiveness in a guiltless Christ? Repentance is certainly a condition of forgiveness. But Christ could not repent. How then could He perfectly meet the conditions of salvation? The answer is that our repentance was latent in that holiness of His which alone could and must create it, as the effect is really part of the cause - that part of the cause which is prolonged in a polar unity into the sequential conditions of time.

Not only, generally, is there an organic moral connection and a spiritual solidarity between Christ and us, but also more particularly, there is such a moral effect on Humanity included in the work of Christ, who causes it, that that antedated action on us, judging, melting, changing us, is also part of His offering to God. He comes bringing His sheaves with Him. In presenting Himself He offers implicitly and proleptically the new Humanity His holy work creates. The judgment we brought on Him becomes our worst judgment when we arraign ourselves; and it makes it so impossible for us to forgive ourselves that we are driven to accept forgiveness from the hands of the very love which our sins doomed to a curse.

What Christ offers to God is, therefore, not simply an objective satisfaction outside His revolutionary effect on the soul of man in the way of faith, repentance, and our whole sanctification. As the very judgment He bore for us is relevant to our sin by His moral solidarity with us, so the value of His work to God includes also that value which it has in acting on us through that same solidarity, and in presenting us to God as the men it makes us to be. He represents before God not a natural Humanity that produces Him as its spiritual classic, but the new penitent Humanity that His influence creates. He calls things that are not yet as though they were. In Him a goodness of ours that is not yet rising from its antenatal spring, brings to naught the sin that is. There was presented to God, in Christ's holiness, also that repentance in us which it alone has power to create. He stretches a hand through time and seizes the far-off interest of our tears. The faith which He alone has power to wake is already offered to God in the offering of all His powers and of His finished work. That obedience of ours which Christ alone is able to create, is already set out in Him before God, implicit in that mighty and subduing holiness of His in which God is always well-pleased. All His obedience and holiness is not only fair and beloved of God, but it is also great with the penitent holiness of the race He sanctifies. Our faith is already present in His oblation. Our sanctification is already presented in our justification. Our repentance is already acting in His confession. The effect of His Cross is to draw us into a repentance which is a dying with Him, and therefore a part of the offering in His death; and then it raises us in newness of life to a fellowship of His resurrection.

He is thus not only the pledge to us of God's love but the pledge to God of our sure response to it in a total change of will and life. We see now how organic, how central to Christ's gospel of Atonement is Paul's idea of dying and rising with Him, how vital to His work is this effect of it, this function of it. For such a process, such an experience, is not a mere moral sequel or echo of ours to the story of the Cross, it is no mere imitation or repetition of its moral greatness; nor is it a sensitive impression of its touching splendor. To die and rise with Christ does not belong to Christian ethic, to the method of Jesus, but it has a far deeper and more religious meaning. It is to be taken into His secret life. It is a mystic incorporation into Christ's death and resurrection as the standing act of spiritual existence. We are baptized into His death, and not merely into dying like Him. We do not echo His resurrection, we share it. As His trophies we become part of Christ's offering to God; just as the captives in his procession were part of the victor's self-presentation to the divinity of Rome. God leadeth us in triumph in Christ (2 Cor. 2:14). It is, indeed, for Christ's sake we are forgiven, but for the sake of a Christ who is the Creator of our repentance and not only the Proxy of our curse. And it is *to* our faith, which is no more perfect than our repentance. It is to nothing so poor as our faith or our repentance that new life is given, but only to Christ on His Cross, and to us for His sake who is the Creator and Fashioner of both. Our justification rests on this atoning creative Christ alone. And when the matter is so viewed, the objection some have to the phrase "for Christ's sake" should disappear.

No martyrdom could do what the death of Christ does for faith. No martyrdom could offer God in advance the souls of a changed race. For no martyr as such is sure of the future. It is easier to forget all the martyrs that the Savior; and their power fades with time, while His grows with the ages. With the martyr's death we can link many admirable reflections, exhortations, and even inspirations. What it does not give us is the new and Eternal Life. It is not the consummation of God's saving purpose for the world.

* This chapter owes much to Kirn, *Herzog,* xx., Art. "Versohnung."

** Because substitution does not take account of the moral results on the soul, and for a full account of the cause we must include all the effects. To do justice to the whole of Christ's work we must include the Church, and in justification include sanctification.

VII. The Threefold Cord

There are three great aspects of the work of Christ which have in turn held the attention of the Church, and come home with special force to its spiritual situation at a special time. There are:

1. Its triumphant aspect; 2. Its satisfactionary aspect; 3. Its regenerative aspect.

The first emphasizes the finality of our Lord's victory over the evil power of devil; the second, the finality of His satisfaction, expiation, or atonement presented to the holy power of God; and the third the finality of His sanctifying or new-creative influence on the soul of man. The first marked the Early Church, the second the Medieval and Reformation Church, while the third marks the Modern Church.

And if you fall back upon the New Testament, where all the subsequent development of the Church is in the germ, as a philosophy might be packed in a phrase, you will find those three strands wonderfully and prophetically entwined in 1 Cor. 1:30, where it is said that Christ is made unto us (2) justification; (3) sanctification; and (1) redemption. The whole history of the doctrine in the Church may be viewed as the exegesis by time of this great text of the Spirit.

Now, it is not meant that in the period specially marked by one of these aspects the other two were absent. In various of the medieval theologians you find all three. And it is a good test of the native aptitude of any theologian, and of his evangelical grasp, that he should find them all necessary to express the fullness of the vast work, and its adequacy to anything so great and manifold as the soul. But what we do not find in the classic theologians of the past is the co-ordination of the three aspects under one comprehensive idea, one organic principle, corresponding to the complete unity of Christ's person, who did the work. We do not find such a unitary view of the work as we should expect when we reflect that it was the work of a personality so complete as Christ, and so absolute as the God who acted in Christ. Yet we must strive after such a view, by the very nature of our faith. A mere composite or eclectic theology means a distracted faith. A creed just nailed together means Churches that cannot draw together. We cannot, at least the Church cannot, rest healthily upon medley and mortised aspects of the one thing which connects our one soul with the one God in one moral world. We cannot rest in unresolved views of reconciliation. As the reconciliation comes to pervade our whole being, and as we answer it with heart and strength and mind, we become more and more impatient of fragmentary ways of understanding it. We crave, and we move, to see that the first aspect is the condition of the second, and the second of the third, and that they all condition each other in a living interaction.

Now the object I have in view in this lecture is to press a former point as furnishing this unity - that the active and effective principle in the work of Christ was the perfect obedience of holy love which He offered amidst the conditions of sin, death, and judgment. The potent thing was not the suffering but the sanctify, and not they sympathetic confession of our sin so much as the practical confession of God's holiness. This principle (I hope to show) co-ordinates the various aspects which have been distorted by isolation. This one action of the holy Savior's total person was, on its various sides, the destruction of evil, the satisfaction of God, and the sanctification of men. And it is in this moral medium of holiness (if I may so say) that these three effects pass and play into each other with a spiritual interpenetration.

Thus Christ's complete victory over the evil power or principle. His redemption (1), is the obverse of His regenerating and sanctifying effect on us (3). To deliver us from evil is not simply to take us out of hell, it is to take us into heaven. Christ does not simply pluck us out of the hands of Satan, He does so by giving us to God. He does not simply release us from slavery, He commits us in the act to a positive liberty. He does not simply cancel the charge against us in court and bid us walk out of jail, He meets us at the prison-door and puts us in a new way of life. His forgiveness is not simply retrospective, it is, in the same act, the gift of eternal life. Our evil is overcome by good. We are won from sin by an act which at the same time makes us not simply innocent but holy.

So also we must see that the third - our regenerate sanctification - is the condition of the second - the complete satisfaction of God. The only complete satisfaction that can be made to a holy God from the sinful side is the sinner's restored obedience, his return to holiness. Now, the cheap and superficial way of putting that is to say that penitent amendment is the only satisfaction we can give to a grieved God. But future amendment does no more than the duty of the future hour. And rivers of water from our eyes will not wash out the guilt of the past; nor will they undo the evil we have set afloat in souls far gone beyond our reach or control. Yet it remains true that nothing can atone to holiness but holiness. And it must be the holiness of the sinner. It must also be an obedience of the kind required by the whole situation, moral and spiritual. It must be the obedience not of improvement but of reconciliation, not of laborious amendment but of regenerated faith. But faith in what? Faith in One who alone contains in Himself a holy obedience so perfect as to meet the holiness of God on the scale of our sin; but One also who, by the same obedience, has the power to reproduce in man the kind of holiness which alone can please God after all that has come and gone. No suffering can atone. No pain can satisfy a holy God; no death, as death. Yet satisfied He must be; else the freedom of grace becomes but an arbitrary and non-holy thing, a thing instinctive to the divine nature instead of a victory of the divine will. Also consider this: much of your difficulty in connection with satisfaction will yield if you keep in view that what we are concerned with is not the satisfaction of a demand but of a

Person, not of a claim by God but of the heart and soul of God. I know it is easier to discuss and adjust statutory claims than to grasp the manifold action of a living and eternal Person. So I am afraid I must be very theological for a moment and tax you accordingly. The chief reason why so many hate theology is because it taxes; and there is nothing we shrink from like spiritual toil. But let the choice and earnest spirit consider this.

The essence of holiness is God's perfect satisfaction, His perfect repose in eternal fullness. And the Christian plea is that this is Self-satisfaction, in the sublimest sense of the phrase. For us, mostly, the word has an ignoble sense. But that is only because what we meet most is an exclusive self-satisfaction, an individual self-sufficiency. But when we have an entirely inclusive self-satisfaction, an eternal and compete adequate to Himself in the most critical situation, we have the whole native fullness of God blessed for ever, with men beneath the shadow of His wing. The perpetual act of holy God is a perpetual satisfaction or accord between His nature and His will at every juncture, and a satisfaction from His own infinite holy resource - a Self-satisfaction. God is always the author of His own satisfaction; that is to say, His holiness is always equal to its own atonement. God in the Son is the perfect satisfaction and joy of God in the Father; and God holy in the sinful Cross is the perfect satisfaction of God the holy in the sinless heavens. Satisfaction there must be in God's own nature, whether under the conditions of perfect obedience in a harmonious world, or under those of obedience jarred and a world distraught. God has power to secure that the perfect holy obedience of heaven shall not be eternally destroyed by the disobedience of earth. He has power to satisfy Himself, and maintain His holiness infrangible, even in face of a world in arms. But satisfied He must be. For an unsatisfied God, a dissatisfied God, would be no God. He would reflect the distraction of the world, and so succumb to it.

But a holy God could be satisfied by neither pain nor death, but by holiness alone. The atoning thing is not obedient suffering but suffering obedience. He could be satisfied and rejoiced only by hallowing of His name, by perfect and obedient answer to His holy heart from amid conditions of pain, death, and judgment. Holy obedience alone, unto death, can satisfy the Holy Lord.

Now as to this obedience mark two things.

1. It includes (we saw) the idea that in obedience Christ accepted the judgment holiness must pass upon sin, and did so in a way that confessed it as holy from amidst the deepest experience of it, the experience not of a spectator but a victim. His obedience was not merely a fine, perfect, and mighty harmony of His own with God's blessed will; but it was the acceptance on man's behalf of that judgment which sin had entailed, and the confession on man's behalf in a tremendous act that the judgment was good and holy. For the holiness of God makes two demands; first, for an answering holiness in love, and second, for a judgment on those who do not answer but defy. And Christ met both, in one and the same act. He was judged as one who, being made sin, was never sinful, but absolutely well-pleasing to God.

2. And the second point is this: The satisfactory obedience must be obedience from the race that rebelled. Its holiness must atone for its sin. But how can that possibly be? Can it be by mere amendment from us? Can we bring any amendment to atone for the past and secure its remission? Could the race do it? Solidary in its sin by its moral unity, could the race earn a solidary salvation? Could you conceive of mankind as one vast sinful soul repenting with a like unity, turning like the prodigal, and deputing the most illustrious spiritual hero of its number to offer its repentance to God in Jesus Christ? If the supposition were possible, that might indeed be a certain welcome offering made *to* God's holiness; but it would not be made *by* it. It would be something beyond the resources of holiness, and God would not be the Savior. He would accept more sacrifice than He had power to make. And it would make the action of Christ a power conferred on Him by self-saved man instead of inherent in Him from God. His commission would be but to God, not from God. And how should a sinful race offer from its own damaged resources what would satisfy the holiness of God? Or, if repentance could satisfy holiness, how are we to know how much, how deep, repentance would do it, and leave us sure it was done?

The holiness that atones, though it return from the race that rebelled, must therefore be the gift of the holiness atoned. For if holiness cold be satisfied by anything outside itself it would not be absolutely holly. So if holiness can be satisfied with nothing but holiness it can only be with a holiness which itself creates. God alone can create in us the holiness that will please Him. And this He has done in Jesus Christ incarnate. But it is in Jesus Christ as the creator of man's holiness, not as the organ of it, as man's sanctifier, and nor merely man's delegate. Christ is our reconciler because on the Cross He was our redeemer from sin's power into no mere independence or courage or safety, but into real holiness; because the same act that redeems us produces holiness, and presents us in this holiness to God and His communion. The holiness of Christ is the satisfying thing to God, yet not because of the beauty of holiness offered to His sight in the perfect character of Christ. We are not saved either by Christ's ethical character or our own, but by His person's creative power and work on us. Christ's holiness is the satisfying thing to God, because it is not only the means but also the anticipation of our holiness, because it carries all our future holiness latent in it and to God's eye patent; because in His saving act He is the creative power of which our new life is the product. It is not only that Christ conquered for Himself and emerged with His soul for a prey, but, He being what He was, His victory contained ours. If He died all died. It was not only that all the sin of the world, pointed to its worst, could not make Him a sinner. It was that by all the holiness of eternity He had power to make the worst sinners saints. Of course, there is no way to sanctification but by deliverance from sin, by being "unsinned." But no sinful man can "unsin" himself, however he amend.

It can only be done by the creation in him of a new life. It can only be done by the sinless Son of God, who lived from eternity in God's holiness, entered man, lived that holiness out in the face of sin, and thus not only broke the evil power by living it down but created that holiness in us by living it in. What is our redemption is thus also our reconciliation. If the atoning thing is holiness (which it is), and not suffering (which it is not), then Christ atoned by an act which created a new holiness in us and not a new suffering. The act which overcame the world intensively for good and all was also the act which slowly masters the world in the extensive sense. His moral and spiritual victory was so deep and thorough that it gives Him power to subdue other consciences to His holy self, world without end.

There is an old word used in this connection which there is much disposition at the present to recall and reclaim. It is the word *surety*, of which some of our fathers were so fond. The word substitute has unfortunate and misleading suggestions, and it has practically been dropped in favor of a word more ethical and more constitutional, like representative. But even that word misleads us to think of Christ as the spiritual protagonist of a democracy, drawing His power from those He represents; and it muffles the truth that His relation to us is royal and not elective, that it is creative and not merely expository. He does not express the natural repentance of the old humanity but creates the penitent faith of the new - "the new man created unto holiness." It is not easy to find a word that has no defect, since all words, even the greatest, are made from the dust and spring from our sandy passions, earthly needs, and fleeting thoughts; and they are hard to stretch to the measure of eternal things without breaking under us somewhere. The word surety itself gives way at a great strain - as does guarantee. Christ's function for us was not simply an assurance to God, from one who knew us well, that for all our aberrations we were sound and could be trusted at bottom. His confession of us was not simply His expression of His conviction, as deep as life, that man, though tough and slow, would in the long-run turn, obey, and confess if properly treated from above. It was not a pledge to God, or an encouragement to man, that Humanity would come right when experience had done its work on his native goodness and his spiritual nature, so much deeper than his sin. It was not a warranty to God that human nature would at last recover its spiritual balance, of which recovery Christ might point to Himself as being an earnest, a prelude, a classic illustration. It was not that Christ staked His insight into the deep nature of this most excellent creature man that he would one day rise from his swine, and return from his rebellion, and fall into the Father's arms. Such poor suggestions as these spring from our common and commercial use of a word like surety or guarantee. As if Christ were a third party between two who did not quite believe in each other. As if God by this aid might be led to foresee that man would come to himself in a faith and repentance distant but certain, might credit it to him in advance, but might pardon on that ground. That would destroy grace. And it would give man the satisfaction of satisfying God if He would but give him time to collect the wherewithal.

Christ is no third party, no arbitrator, no moral broker. And He is not the first installment of man's return to God, its harbinger. In no such sense is He our surety before God. Because His work is not one of insight but of regeneration. It did not turn on His genius for reading us, but His power to create us anew. He Himself is the creator in us of what He promises for us. Any surety that Christ gives to God for man is really God swearing by Himself; it is the Creator's self-assurance of His own regenerative power. Christ, as the Eternal Son of Holy God, can offer Him a holiness which creates and includes that of the race, and does not simply prophesy it.

We might put it thus: Christ alone in His sinless perfection can feel all God's holiness in judging sin; and therefore He alone could confess and honor it. No sinful man could do that; and therefore no sinful man could duly repent. The value of repentance is always in proportion to the sense of God's holiness. To confess that holiness is the great postulate in order to confess sin. And the race cold duly confess its sin and repent only if there arose in it One who by a perfect and impenitent holiness in Himself, and by His organic unity with us, could create such holiness in the sinful as should make the new life one long repentance transcended by faith and thankful joy. This was and is Christ's work. And the satisfaction to God, as it was certainly not His suffering, was also more than the spectacle of His own holy soul presented to God. It was that holy soul (the holier as He faced and conquered evil ever growing more black and bitter) - it was that holy soul seen by God as the cause and creator of the race's confession, both of holiness and of sin, in a Church of the reborn. The satisfaction to God was Christ, not as an isolated character, or in an act wholly outside us and our responsive union with Him; but it was Christ as the author of our sanctification and repentance. Our repentance and our sanctity are of saving value before God only as produced by the creative holiness of Christ. Christ creates our holiness because of His own sanctification of Himself - John 17:19 - and His complete victory over the evil power in a life-experience of moral conflict.

You wish perhaps here to ask me this question: Is then the sanctity of a Unitarian who rejects any satisfaction by Christ, any atonement, as the ground of man's holiness, is that sanctity of no account before God? Is the true repentance of those who do not know of an atoning Christianity of little price with Him? Far from it. But from our point of view we must regard them as incomplete stages, which draw their value with God from a subliminal union with that completed and holy offering of Christ which He never ceases to see, however far it be beneath our conscious light.

When therefore we speak of Christ as our Surety, we mean much more than would be meant by a mere sponsorship. We suppose a solidary union of faith created by the Savior in the sinner, which not only impresses him but incorporates him with Christ. All turns upon that spiritual solidarity. All turns upon the reality of that new life for which Paul had to invent a new phrase - "in Christ." A tremendous phrase, like that other, "the New Creation" - and hardly intelligible to a youthful or impressionist Christianity. The real ground of our forgiveness is not our confession of sin, and not even Christ's confession of our sin, but His agonized confession of God's holiness, and its absorbing effect on us. To be in grace we must be found in Him. Our new penitent life is His creation. He contains the principle and power of our forgiveness. And it comes home to us only as we abide in Him. In Him, and only in Him, the normal holy man, the man holy with all the holiness of God, have we the living power of release from guilt, escape from sin, repentance, faith, and newness of life. We are justified only as we are incorporate (not clothed) in the perfect righteousness of Christ, our Regenerator, and not in proportion as the righteousness of Christ has made palpable way in us. It is not as Christ is in us that we are saved, but as we are in Christ. It is this being in Christ for our justification that makes justification necessarily work out to sanctification, and forgiveness be one with eternal life.

We shall be misled even by what is true in the representative aspect of Christ unless we grasp how much more He is, how creative He is, how the solidarity involved in His representation is due to His own act of self-identification and not to natural identity with us. We must take quite seriously that supreme word of a "new creation in Jesus Christ." We need not get lost in discussing the metaphysic of it; but we must have so tasted the new life that nothing but the strongest word possible is just to it.

Christ our New Creator! He was not simply a new departure n the history of *ethical civilization*, by the introduction of an exalted morality. If that was what He came with, He brought much less than the conscience needs; and on countless points He has left us without guidance today. Nor was He simply a great new departure in the history of *religious ideas*. He did much more than bring us a new idea of God. If that was all, again it was not what we need. For we have more and higher ideas of God than we know what to do with, more than we have power to realize. But He stands for a new departure in the history of *Creation*. His work in so far is cosmic. It is a new story added to the world. It is a new departure in the action which made the universe. It is an entirely new stage in the elevation of human nature, so imperfect in our first creation, to its divine height in holiness. By His moral treatment of our sinful case, which is our actual historic case, we are taken into a share of His superhuman life. That is our salvation. It is life and power we need. It is to be made over again by the Maker's redeeming hand. We are redeemed *from* the ban of sin's magic circle by the only One who has the secret of the unseen powers; we are joined with the sin-destroying life of Christ. And we are redeemed, by the very nature of that redemption, *into* the fellowship of His eternal and blessed peace. And that is our Reconciliation. The act that justified sanctifies and reconciles. And that totality of Christ in His Church is what God looks on and is satisfied. We are, as a believing race, in the Son in whom He is always well pleased.

Now what is it that has created so much difficulty for the old Protestant doctrine? I mean difficulty in the mind of Christian believers, and still more in their experience. For we need not trouble here about difficulty from the side of the worldlings or the ethical sentimentalists. But difficulty arose within the pale of the most devout and devoted evangelical experience. Perhaps it has arisen in your own minds. Well, the old Protestantism, as you know, was greatly exercised about the true relation between faith and works. And it had to insist so strongly on the sole value of faith in order to cope with Rome that its later years fell into an excessive dread of good works, lest there should be ascribed to them saving effect. As a result faith was credited with a merely receptive power, or no more beyond that than a power of assent. Men lost hold of the great Lutheran fact that faith is the most mighty and active thing in the soul, that our faith is our all before God, that it is an energy of the whole person, that good works are done by this whole believing person, and that faith by its very nature, as trust in God's love, is bound to work out in love. They misread the moral impulse in faith, its power to recast personality and refashion life. They did not, of course, overlook the necessity of such renovation; but they put it down to a subsequent action of the Spirit over and above faith - almost as if the Spirit and His sanctification were a second revelation, a new dispensation. Which indeed many of the mystics thought it was - like many rationalist mystics today, who think we have outgrown historic Christianity and the historic Christ through our modern light. The old Protestant orthodoxy did not realize that the real source of the Spirit is the Cross. It therefore detached faith from life in a way that has produced the most unfortunate results, both in an antinomianism within the Church, and in a Socinian protest without, which was inevitable, and so far valuable, but was equally extreme. Faith was treated by the positive school then as a mystic power, or an intellectual, but not as a moral. It was not the renovating power in life, but only prepared the ground for the renovating power to come in. It had not in itself the transforming power either individually or socially. Its connection with love was accidental and not necessary - as it must be, being faith in love.

Now, if we translate this experimental language into theological, it means that they did not connect up justification and sanctification. Forgiveness of sin was not identified closely enough with eternal life. Eternal life was detached from identity with that which was the true eternal in life, from faith's practical (*i.e.,* experimental) godliness. Forgiveness did not go, as it should, with renewal of heart and conduct in one act. It delivered from an old world without opening a new and planting us in its revolutionized principles. Faith had, indeed, the power to do works of love, but it was not driven to them so that it could do no other. And this flaw in faith corresponded to a like flaw in the reading of Christ's act which was the object of faith. They treated the work of Christ in a way far too objective. It was something done wholly over our heads. There was not a solidary connection between Christ's work and the Church it created. Attention was concentrated upon one aspect of Christ's work - its action on God. That is quite an essential aspect (perhaps the chief), but it must not be isolated. No aspect of that work must be isolated, as I began by saying. It is the service an accomplished theology does for the Church to keep all aspects in one purview, in the proportion of a great and comprehensive faith. We have today gone to another extreme, and isolated another aspect - the moral effect of Christ on man. So we need not give ourselves any airs of superiority to the old orthodoxy in that respect of one-sidedness. And we must also remember that the whole secret of truth in this matter is not what we are sometimes told - a change of emphasis. We have changed the emphasis, and yet we are short of the truth; and the state of the Church's piety shows it. We have moved the accent from the objective to the subjective work of Christ; and we fall victims more and more to a weak religious subjectivism which has the ethical interest but no the moral note. We fall into a subjectivism which is reflected in one aspect of Pragmatism and overworks the principle contained in the words, "By their fruits shall y know them" (know *them*, whether they are true to the Gospel, not the Gospel and whether it is true to God and reality). So that people say, "I will believe whatever I feel does me good. My soul will eat what I enjoy, and drink what makes me happy." They are their own test of truth, and "their own Holy Ghost." The secret, therefore, is not change of accent but balance of aspects. And the true and competent theology is not only one which regards the Church's whole history and outlook (thinking in centuries, I called it), but it is one disciplined to think in proportion, to think together the various aspects of the Cross, and make them enrich and not exclude one another.

The defect of the old view was, then, as I have said, that it could not couple up justification and sanctification. It could not show how the same act of Christ which delivered from the guilt of sin delivered also from its power. And this was because in the justification too much stress was laid upon the suffering; and suffering in itself has no sanctifying power. You see how our practical experience, when it is well noted, provides our theological principles. We do find that suffering by itself debases, and even imbrutes, instead of purifying; that pain is an occasion rather than a cause of profit. That is a moral principle of spiritual experience. Consequently when excessive attention was given to the suffering of Christ, and the atoning value was supposed to reside there instead of in the holy obedience, the work of Christ lost in purifying and sanctifying effect, whatever it may have done in pacifying or converting. The atoning thing being the holy obedience to the Holy, the same holiness which satisfied God sanctifies us. That is the idea the Reformers did not grasp through their preoccupation with Christ's sufferings. But it is the only idea which unites justification and sanctification and both with redemption. For the holiness which satisfied God and sanctifies us also destroyed the evil power in the world and its hold on us. It was the moral conquest of the world's evil, amid the extreme conditions of sin and suffering, by a Victor who had a capital solidarity with the race, and not merely an individual connection with it as a member. So that it has been said that we must explain and correct current ideas of substitutionary expiation by the idea of solidary reparation. The curse on man was the guilty power of sin and its train - hitherto invincible. There was but one way in which this could be mastered. A moral curse could be mastered only in a purely moral way, the world-curse by the world-conscience. It could be mastered but by One whose sinlessness was not only negatively proof against all that sin could do, but positively holy; and He was thus deadly to sin, satisfactory to God's loving judgment, and creative of a new humanity in the heart of the old. This was a task beyond mere substitutionary penal suffering as that phrase is now so poorly understood. For that would have been just and effectual only if it had fallen on the arch-rebel, who, with the nobility of Milton's Satan in his first stage, assumed himself all the worst consequences of his revolt to spare the other souls whom he had misled.

The truth is that Anselm, in spite of the unspeakable service he did both to the faith and thought of his time and all time, yet put theology on a false track in this matter. He had too much to say of a superethical tribute paid to God's *honor* by the composition of a voluntary suffering. Our sin was compounded rather than really atoned. He did not grasp the sacrifice of Christ as made to God's *holiness*; as one therefore which could only be ethical in its nature, by way of holy obedience. This obedience was the Holy Father's joy and satisfaction. He found Himself in it. And it was also the foiling and destruction of the evil power. And it was farther the creative source of holiness in a race not only impressed by the spectacle of its tragic hero victorious, but regenerate by the solidarity of a new life from its creative Head. The work of Christ was thus in the same act triumphant on evil, satisfying to the heart of God, and creative to the conscience of man by virtue of His solidarity with God on the one side, and on the other with the race. He subdued Satan, rejoiced the Father, and set up in Humanity the kingdom - all in one supreme and consummate act of His one person. He destroyed the kingdom of evil, not by way of preparation for the kingdom of God, but by actually establishing God's kingdom in the heart of it. And He rejoiced, filled, and satisfied the heart of God, not by a statutory obedience, or by one private to Himself, which spectacle disposed God to bless and sanctify man; but by presenting in the compendious compass of His own person a Humanity presanctified by the irresistible power of His own creative and timeless work.

The holy demand of God is always couched in a false form when it is made to call for the expiation of an equivalent suffering instead of a confession of God's holiness, adequately holy, from the side of the sinner under judgment. Heaven and its happiness are wrongly conceived as immunity from judgment instead of joy in the consummation of judgment in righteousness and holiness for ever. It was not clear to the old view that the very nature of justification was sanctification, that the Justifier was so only as One who always perfectly sanctified Himself, and was organic, in the act, with the race in its new life. It appeared to our fathers as if sanctification were only a facultative sequel of justification.

Whatever we mean, therefore, by substitution, it is something more than merely vicarious. It is certainly not something done over our heads. It is representative. Yet not by the will of man choosing Christ, but by the will of Christ choosing man, and freely identifying Himself with man. It is a matter not so much of substitutionary expiation (which, as these words are commonly understood, leaves us too little committed), but of solidary confession and praise from amid the judgment fires, where the Son of God walks with the creative sympathy of the holy among the sinful sons of men. It is not as if Christ were our changeling, as if His lot and ours were transposed on the Cross. But He was our self-appointed plenipotentiary, and what He engaged for we must implement by an organic spiritual entail. So far His work was as objective as our creation, as independent of our leave; and it committed us without reference to our consent but to our need. When He died for all, all implicitly died. The great transaction was done for the race. But objective as it was, gift as it was to us from pure grace, it was so in its initiative rather than in its method. Essentially it was a new creation of us, but practically the new creator was in us, and the word was flesh. In such a way that He and His are one by faith in a solidarity corresponding from beneath, *mutatis mutandis,* to the solidarity between Father and Son from above.

He and His form an organic spiritual unity - one will in two parties or persons. Mere substitution is mere exchange of parts, in which one is excluded and immune. But the work of Christ is inclusive and committal, by our continuity of life with Him through the spirit in a Church. * The suffering of Christ is but the under and seamy side of that solidarity whose upper side is the beauty of our corporate holiness in Him. The same law, the same act, which laid our sin on Him lays His holiness on us, and absorbs us into His satisfaction to God. In the same act God made Him to be sin for us and made us righteousness in Him. In the empirical sense we are no more made righteous than He was made sinful. But we are as closely incorporated in the holy world as He was in the sinful. And our holiness is not ours, in the same sense as our sin was not His - in the sense of initiative and individual responsibility for it.

It was as our self-appointed representative that Christ died. He died as the result, as the finale, of the act by which He identified Himself with us and emptied Himself from heaven. He is our Head by divine right and not by election of ours. Our representative, our surety He was - not our choice illustration, not our mandatory champion, not our moral deputy, not our friendly sponsor promising that we should one day pay our debt because of His optimistic faith in us. It was not in us that He had faith so much as in Himself as the power and grace of God. He did not promise that we would pay (if the metaphor may be allowed); He paid for us, knowing that in Himself alone could we raise the vast advance. What was presented to God was not only Christ's perfection, nor was it His confidence in us, but also His antedated action on us, His confidence in Himself for us. That was what stood to our good. There was offered to God a racial obedience which was implicit in the creative power of His, and not merely parallel with His, as if He were our first fruits instead of our Sun.

The juristic aspect is a real element in Christ's death. It has a moral core; and we cannot discard it without discarding the moral order of the world as one revelation of that irrefragable holiness of God which must be expressed in judgment and confessed from its midst. The chief defect of the great revolution which began in Schleiermacher and ended in Ritschl has been that it allowed no place to that side of Christ's work. And it is a defect that much impoverishes the current type of religion, beclouds it, and robs it of the power of moral conviction by reducing the idea of sin and dismissing the note of guilt. It makes grace not so much free as arbitrary, because it does not regard in its revelation what is due to the holiness of God. It banishes from our Christian faith the one note which more than any other we have today come to need restored - the note of judgment. When properly construed the juristic element is a great power to life faith from the mere ethicism to which Ritschl tends into the mystic region which is so essential to make a moral power a religious, to provide a home for the soul as well as a lamp to our feet, and to secure for believers a hidden communion with Christ. It also saves the grace of God from being a mere favoritism to believers, or a mere concession to misery.

There is no doubt we are in reaction from a time when that side of things was overdone. The juristic aspect taken alone, and taken in relation to legal demand rather than personal holiness - such *satisfaction*, when isolated, does not do justice to the aspect in which Christ was triumphant over evil (*redemption*) nor to the aspect in which His work is regenerative for mankind (*sanctification*). And it tended to promote the fatal notion that holiness could be satisfied with suffering and death, or with anything short of an answering holiness effected and guaranteed. The satisfaction in it was offered to a distributive justice rather than to a personal holiness, to a claim rather than a person, to a regulative law rather than to a constitutive life. All that and more is quite true.

But I must ask you to deal sympathetically with those juristic views, to treat them with spiritual insight. It was the vice of Socinianism, and it is the vice of the Rationalism which is its legatee, that it criticized orthodoxy by the fierce light of the natural conscience instead of by the inner nature and better knowledge of the relation on which orthodoxy founded all. It criticized theology by the natural reason and not by the supernatural Gospel. There is nothing more vulgar than slashing criticism in such a matter. You cannot slash here without cutting the face of some great and true saints to whom these views are dearer than life because bound up with their entrusted Gospel and their life eternal. One of the most damnatory features of popular theological liberalism is the violent handling of what it calls orthodoxy, and its total lack of spiritual flexibility and interpretative sympathy - caused largely by the prior lack of theological knowledge and culture. That some orthodoxy is also shallow and insolent is no justification for those whose plea is that they know better. I pray you to listen to the old theology not as fools but as wise, as evolutionists and reformers, not as dynamitards. Consider what was gained for us in it. True, it sometimes presented its gain in false forms, as when it spoke of the equivalence of Christ's suffering to what we all deserved. That was but the form, and the Socinians did good work in the correction of such things. But this at least had been gained - the conviction that it was not the touchy honor of a feudal monarch that was to be dealt with at the had of the world, but the love of a just God. The conviction behind all was the grandest moral conviction possible - that all things are by Christ in the hands of infinite righteousness and holy love. This vast moral step had been taken. Men had come to realize that the result of Christ's work was eternal *right*; and especially that it was right, not in reference to the claims of an evil will, but in regard to those of a will perfectly good. The days were certainly outgrown by this juristic theology when there could be any such talk as filled the early Church about dealing with the rights Satan had won over man. Evil has no rights in the soul. From that, indeed, it was a great advance even to Anselm's apotheosis of God's honor. And it was a further advance still beyond feudal dignity when the great and noble categories of juris-prudence were invoked to replace the notion of courtly or military honor which made God and man duelists rather than ought else. It was a vast step in the moralizing of theology when its grand concern came to be the establishment of men before a righteous and social judge. Do not speak contemptuously of that step. It is one of our own stages. It gave us rest and uplifting on our journey to where we now stand. We have only had to carry further that moralizing of the nature of justice. The whole idea was ethical and social compared with what went before it - at least as much so as ours now marks a farther advance. It was ethical as regards claims by an evil power which can have no moral rights. And it was social in that it brought Christian belief into line with the ruling principles of society as it then was. It is a view, moreover, which has shown itself capable of inspiring some of the deepest, sweetest, and most beneficent piety the world has ever seen. Moreover, it had in it active conditions of moral growth which broke through the packthreads of its own time. We today have only had to carry forward that process of moralizing the idea of our relation to God which the jurists began. Their theology had a moral passion which shed the features in it that were ethically defective, and assimilated the moral idea of the Gospel as we are now taught to read it in a Bible rediscovered and reconstrued by the Spirit's action both in the faith and the criticism of the day.

Among these three aspects of Christ's work some minds will be drawn by preference to one, some to another, just as different ages have been. Some souls, according to their experience, will gravitate to the great Deliverance, some to the great Atonement, and some to the great Regeneration. Some ministries will be marked by the influence of one, some of another. That is all within the free affinities of the spiritual life, and the preferential sympathies of the moral idiosyncrasy. And the Church is enriched by the complementary action of such diversities of ministry. But what ought not to be encouraged is any tendency on the part of those who prefer the one line to deny the equal right of the others. And what ought not to be tolerated is the habit of denunciation, by those who see the one side, of the sides they find nothing in; and especially the habit of assuming that the sides they are blind to represent a lower Christian level. Where this is possible there has really been little done for the conscience by the view that is adopted. And it is both absurd and overweening to ask us to believe that those sections of the Church, and those lights of piety, who held to views at present in the background were all theological bigots and moral inepts; that real moral aptitude and theological faculty did not arise till now; that a like devotion obscures such questions; that babes and suckling perfect theological praise; that wisdom is justified by children; and that it is now the monopoly of those who detach theology from religion, and dismiss it to a historical museum.

If Christ by the Savior of the world in any sense, the thing He did must be at least as great as the world. And if as great, then no less manifold, and no less the object for first-rate intelligence than the lower objects of experience. Faith in such a Savior cannot continue to live for either heart or conscience if it is detached from mind.

Nor can mind submit to be warned off the supreme object of the soul's concern if that object is loved and sought with all our heart and soul and strength. The very type of prayer in the non-theological forms which claim to be Christian shows to what we can sink when faith is stripped of mind and strength. It is only a poor Christ that can be housed in a poor creed, and a feeble prophet that is canonized when a sentimentalized ethic is offered as religion.

* In His saving act He so became one with the race that the new Humanity He set up arises in history as the company of those who answer and seal His incarnate act with their faith. By his incarnation and redemption Christ did not simply deify Humanity, as a pagan Christianity had it in the fourth century, nor manifest the essential deity of Humanity as a pagan Christianity has it in the twentieth. But He so took a Humanity predestined for Him that those who take Him should become the new Humanity in the true Church.

Addendum

There is a point in chapter iv where, in speaking freely, I have spoken loosely, and I have expressed myself with some want of caution likely to cause misunderstanding of my full meaning. I there say that the wrath of God is not to be taken as a pathos or affection, but as the working out of His judgment in a moral order. My intention was to discourage the idea that it was a mood or temper, and to connect it with the sure changelessness of God's moral nature. But on reviewing the passage I find I have so put it that I might easily suggest that the anger of God was simply the automatic recoil of His moral order upon the transgressor, the nemesis which dogs him and makes hard his way, his self-hardening; as if there were no personal reaction of a Holy God Himself upon the sin, and no infliction of His displeasure upon the sinner. This is an impression I should be sorry to leave; for it is one that would take much of its most holy significance and solemn mystery out of the work of Christ.

Was Christ's bearing of God's wrath just His exposure to the action of the vast moral machine? Did He just become involved, as our rescuer, in the mechanism which regulates ethical Humanity, using at times man's anger as its agent? This mechanism might be there possibly without the ordinance of a God that it should be so, or possibly as the institution of a deist and distant God who calmly watches His world spin with the motion He gave it. But is God not personally immanent and active in His own moral order? Did Christ just incur the automatic penalty of that order as He strove to save its victims? Was He just caught in the works? Or was there implied, and felt, also the element of personal displeasure acting through that order - the element that would differentiate wrath from mere nemesis, and infliction from mere recoil?

Granting then that there was in Christ's suffering the element of personal displeasure and infliction, was it man's or God's? Was His treatment simply the reaction of sinful man against holiness, or was it the reaction of a holy God against sin? Did He Himself feel He was yielding to man's dark will, or God's will, darker, but higher and surer? Did He suffer, just as the holiest saint might in a wicked world, the extreme hate of men; or was God's displeasure also upon Him? We have abundantly seen that this could not be upon Him as His own desert, not as it lies upon a guilty conscience. If He was made sin He was not made sinful; if He was made a curse He was not accursed. And have we not also seen that He who acted in our stead could act with no fitness and no precision if He took on Him the mere equivalent of what the guilty would have paid had they never been redeemed (that would have needed a generous arch-rebel), but only if he paid what was appointed as the price of their redemption? The uttermost farthing is not the last mite of their desert but of God's ransom price. But the curse of sin's sequel is most real whatever the amount. And it was certainly on Christ, by His freely putting Himself under it beside the men on whom it lay. That curse then - was it an infliction from God, which did not lift, did not cease to be inflicted, even when the Son put Himself in its way; or was it something that struck Him only from men below and not from God above at all?

Surely as it falls on man at least it is God's infliction. We do not only grieve God but we provoke His anger. There is nothing we need more to recall into our sense of sin at present than this (though we must extend it, as we must extend our redemption, to a racial and solidary wrath of God in which we share). Its absence has slackened and flattened the whole tone and level of Christian life. The love of God becomes real anger to our sin, and to us as we identify ourselves with the sin, to us while, outside Christ, we are no more than members of a sinful race. Is not our satisfaction and increase in well-doing the personal blessing of God? Then surely our misery and infatuation on the other path is His personal anger. If a true evolution carries with it the personal and joyful action of God in blessing its results, is the result of degeneration a mere natural process in the moral region, secluded from God's displeased action and infliction? Is it all His will only as a thing willed, and not as His action in willing it?

Weigh, as men of real moral experience, what is involved in the hardening of the sinner. That is the worst penalty upon sin, its cumulative and deadening history. Well, is it simply self-hardening? Is it simply the reflex action of sin upon character, sin going in, settling in, and reproducing itself there? Is it no part of God's positive procedure in judging sin, and bringing it, for salvation, to a crisis of judgment grace? When Pharaoh hardens his heart, is that in no sense God hardening Pharaoh's heart? When a man hardens himself against God, is there nothing in the action and purpose of God that takes part in that induration? Is that anger not as really as the superabounding grace? Are not both bound up in one complex treatment of the moral world? When a man piles up his sin and rejoices in iniquity, is God simply a bystander and spectator of the process? Does not God's pressure on the man blind him, urge him, stiffen him, shut him up into sin, if only that he might be shut up to mercy alone? Is it enough to say that this is but the action of a process which God simply watches in a permissive way? Is He but passive and not positive to the situation? Can the Absolute be passive to anything? If so, where is the inner action of the personal god whose immanence in things is one of His great modern revelations? Everything you call absolute is in active relation to the whole creation. Go into the psychology of sin as it is understood, not indeed today, but by those in the long, deep history of the moral soul whose experience coincided with a real genius for reading it - true sons of him of Romans 7. Ask such experients if it is never thus - that the anger of God promotes a sin, cherished in the private imagination, to actual transgression; which then shocks, appalls, the dallier into the horrified loss of all confidence in the flesh; that out of the collapse may rise a totally new man? God never put sin in the world; but, sin being in the world, with its spreading power, does God never bring it to such a head as precipitates its destruction? Does He never drive the lunatic over a precipice into water where he can be saved and divert him from the quarry edge where he would be dashed to pieces? Did God not so act with Israel (John 12:39)? When sin has once begun, is there no such thing morally possible as the provocative action of God's law? With God's law sin gains life (Romans 7:10) and becomes more sinful. Every law deepens the guilt of defying it. That is the curse of the law. And is that law detached from God, and cut adrift to do its own mechanic work under His indifference? Is it not His curse and anger still, if God be in His law, as we now do believe Him to pervade His world?

The love of God is not more real than the wrath of God. For He can be really angry only with those He loves. And how can Absolute Love love without acting to save?

Well, if it be so, that God's direct displeasure and infliction is the worst thing in sin's penalty, did the displeasure totally vanish from the infliction when Christ stood under it? Would He have really borne the true judgment on sin if it had? Was Christ's great work not the meeting of that judgment and hallowing it? Did the complete acceptance of God's displeasure as an essential factor in the curse? A holy God could not look on sin without acting on it; nor could He do either but to abhor and curse it, even when His Son was beneath it. Wherein is guilt different from sin but in this - that it is sin, not cut adrift from God and let go its own way and go to pieces, but sin placed under the anger of God, under the personal reaction of that Absolute Holy God which no creature, no situation, can escape? And could Christ bear our guilt and take it away if He did not carry it there, and bear it there, and hallow its judgment there? Did He just throw it down there, leave it, and rid Himself of it? Does not the best of sons suffer from the angry gloom that spreads from the father over the whole house at the prodigal's shameless shame? Did God not lay on Him the iniquity of us all, and inflict that veiling of His face which darkened to dereliction even the Redeemer's soul? It is not desert that is the worst thing in judgment, but desertion - the sense of desert forsaken by God. The forsakenness is the worst judgment. For with God's presence my sense of desert may be my sanctification. What Christ bore was not simply a sense of the connection between the sinner and the impersonal consequences of sin, but a sense of the sinner's relation to the personal *vis-a-vis* of an angry God. God never left Him, but He did refuse Him His face. The communion was not broken but its light was withdrawn. He was forsaken but not disjoined. He was insolubly bound to the very Father who turned away and could not look on sin but to abhor and curse it even when His Son was beneath it. How could He feel the grief of being forsaken by God if He was not at bottom one with Him? Neglect by one to whom we have no link makes no trouble.

Even a theologian so little orthodox as Weizsacker says: -

"The moral experience of guilt is too strong to let me say that it can be met by any mere manifestation of grace or of love from God to man - even when that manifestation carries in it the sympathetic suffering of sin's curse, borne merely in the way of confirming the manifestation and pressing the object-lesson." "When repentance helps the believer to peace it is not *ex opere operato*, because he has repented and may now trust grace; but it is because in his repentance he has part and lot in the infinite pain and confession of Christ."

www.ingramcontent.com/pod-product-compliance
Lightning Source LLC
Chambersburg PA
CBHW071318040426
42444CB00009B/2043